OH CRAP!
POTTY
TRAINING

OH CRAP! POTTY TRAINING

EVERYTHING MODERN PARENTS NEED TO KNOW TO DO IT ONCE AND DO IT RIGHT

Jamie Glowacki

GALLERY BOOKS

New York London Toronto Sydney New Delhi

G

Gallery Books
An Imprint of Simon & Schuster, LLC
1230 Avenue of the Americas
New York, NY 10020

This Gallery Books trade paperback edition May 2024

GALLERY BOOKS and colophon are registered trademarks of
Simon & Schuster, LLC

Simon & Schuster: Celebrating 100 Years of Publishing in 2024

For information about special discounts for bulk purchases,
please contact Simon & Schuster Special Sales at
1-866-506-1949 or business@simonandschuster.com.

The Simon & Schuster Speakers Bureau can bring authors to
your live event. For more information or to book an event,
contact the Simon & Schuster Speakers Bureau at
1-866-248-3049 or visit our website at www.simonspeakers.com.

Interior design by Kathryn A. Kenney-Peterson

Manufactured in the United States of America

10 9 8 7 6 5 4 3 2 1

Library of Congress Cataloging-in-Publication Data has been applied for.

ISBN 978-1-6680-5001-9
ISBN 978-1-5011-2299-6 (ebook)

CONTENTS

INTRODUCTION

Welcome to *Oh Crap! Potty Training*. This is not only the definitive guide to potty training, it's super special—the tenth anniversary revision of this book! Yay! It's such an honor to be able to revise this book with all that I've learned in the past decade.

I'm not just an author. I work full time with parents, troubleshooting every potty problem imaginable. I am regularly learning new things so it's a joy to be able to update this book. Also, a lot has changed in the world in the past decade. For example, when I first wrote it, I had never worked with a single dad, so the book was written for moms. But now, more than ever before, dads are taking part in the potty process, sometimes even completely running the potty show. For brevity, I'll do my best to use the word *parents*. I typically do see a primary caregiver, no matter what the family situation is.

I used to call this a three-day plan. There's a reason there are a million "three-day potty training methods" out there on the Internet. It takes roughly three days for the average child to get over the major hump of potty training. But your child is unique, as is your relationship with them. Every child has their own learning curve, and—this is a big *and*—you have an emotional stake in this. You and your child have a wonderfully strong bond; this is to both your advantage and your disadvantage. So, yes, some bumps can appear

1

on this road. Over the years, I've found that some parents get invested in potty training in three days flat. This, however, creates the very pressure you want to avoid when potty training. If you put pressure on the process, it will collapse.

I'll also throw this in: we all know how very different our children are from one another, and yet somehow the Internet has led us to think that there's a cookie-cutter version of potty training that will work for every kid. Impossible. How could one way work identically on very different people?

Consider what you are reading to be a curriculum. I don't hold the magic keys. You do. I am a potty training expert, but you are the expert on your child. If I say something that doesn't resonate, ditch it. I do my best to back up everything I say with a healthy dose of *why*, but I'm happy to be wrong.

Walking and talking, learning to read and tie shoes and ride bikes are all wonderful milestones that we parents look forward to. Potty training, however, fills many of us with dread. It shouldn't. One of the coolest things I've discovered about potty training is that it's your first glimpse into how your child learns. Every child learns—and therefore potty trains—a little differently, and you get great insight into your child's learning methods and curve.

Over the years, I've come to realize that there really are no "methods" of potty training: to potty train, you must take the diapers off the child. What happens next—your child's reaction to that—is what everyone fears. Rest assured, in this book, I'm going to teach you the most painless way to get your child out of diapers. More importantly, I'm going to present the answers to any questions you might have going forward from that point. The bottom line is that all kids react differently to not wearing a diaper, and that is where the rubber meets the road. We'll get into all the nitty-gritty details soon enough. First, though, I need to do some myth busting, and you need to do some mental prep. Then I'll walk you through the first few days of potty training, and finally, we'll get to all the potential questions you might have.

It will take most kids about three to seven days for the potty training to click. For some kids, the process may be longer, and for others, it will be shorter. You won't know what kind of kid you have until you jump in, but no matter how fast or slow the process is, it's all okay and expected. I cannot state this enough: having a preconceived notion of how long this will take will almost always get you into hot water.

It's really no different from learning to read or other major milestones. Some kids pick it up quickly and seemingly intuitively, while others take longer to string letters together into sounds (the latter is more common). I'm going to give you markers to track progress, because that's what's important here. This whole thing is about progress, not perfection. I'm going to repeat that because it's so important: we are always looking for progress, not perfection. What we are going to be doing is bringing your child's awareness from *Clueless*, to *I Peed*, to *I'm Peeing*, to *I Have to Go Pee*. That's it. it seems so simple when I say it like that. Some kids cruise through one component and stall out on another. Again, you won't know what your kid will do until you jump in.

You'll notice that nothing here is written in stone as an absolute. We are dealing with little human beings. Their brains aren't mature yet, but these little people are very capable of thinking their own thoughts, and they come chock-full of their own personalities. I'm passionate about potty training because of the many differences between one child and another, so having said that, you need to keep your child's individual personality in the front of your mind as you go through this process.

And a little last bit of housekeeping before we jump in: because I'm constantly learning new things, I wish this book could be a living document. Unfortunately, that's not how publishing works. As of this writing, I keep current on my two podcasts: *Oh Crap! Potty Training* and *Oh Crap! Parenting*. I maintain a YouTube channel and a lively Instagram page. You can also get all things through jamieglowacki.com, including private consultations if you need them.

I mention clients and specific situations throughout. For privacy, all names have been changed. I've also blended various scenarios for brevity. Please be sure to read the whole book, especially the questions and answers toward the end of chapter 17.

I do cuss and that makes some people mad. My humor is twisted and I'm pretty sarcastic. I assure you, it's not out of disrespect. I make my living talking about poop; I have to have some levity. I don't mean to offend, and I don't take such a major milestone lightly. Still, sometimes no word other than "f**k" will do.

I'm thrilled you've chosen me to help you on this journey.

I don't take your trust lightly. With that . . . LFG . . . !

CHAPTER 1

In the Beginning . . .

First off, although I'll admit that I really like the word *crap*, I tend to use *pee* and *poop* with my own child, and those are the words I'll use in this book. I think they are pretty commonplace and fit the bill nicely. Of course, don't feel you have to use them. You should decide on your own family's lingo. Any words will do, as long as there is consistency.

I'll be talking about mixed messages quite a lot. We send our children many mixed messages about potty training, and I think that's one of the reasons it's become such a huge ordeal. The words you use are just one example. I don't care if you choose to say *poop*, *crap*, *she-she*, *urine*, *BM*, *peeps*, *caca*, *doody*, *lala*, *foofoo*, or anything else. Just be consistent. Bear in mind that this word will be said *very loudly* in church, at the library, in the market. Be sure it's a word you are comfortable with at high volume and frequency. I've worked with parents who say "caca" at home and then try to get away with "BM" in public. The toddler mind doesn't work that way. Don't confuse the issue.

I know some parents object to the term *potty training*. I've heard it said that training is for animals, not children. Let's just agree that "training" is synonymous with "learning" for our purposes. After all, even as an adult, you "train" in something in order to learn it. As an analogy, when you get a new job, you receive training: someone already skilled guides you through your new duties. Most likely, you are clearly told what is expected of you and shown how to do it. When you make mistakes, your boss gently tells you what you did wrong and how to do it right. After a certain amount of time, you're expected to have mastered your new duties. There you go—that's potty training.

I also like to compare potty training to learning to walk. I've always been amazed by kids learning to walk. Let's face it—they get around much faster by crawling, so why take on this new skill? Because it's in our nature as humans to walk upright. It's also in our nature to pee and poop in designated areas. Even cultures that don't have plumbing have definitive places for excrement.

Think back to when your child learned to walk. You probably watched her constantly to make sure she didn't whack her head on something. You put her between your legs and held her hands and helped her along. You cheered her on and smothered her with kisses. You showed off her new skill to anyone who set foot in your house. When she fell and cried, you picked her up, dusted her off, and encouraged her to try again. Did you give her stickers or M&M's for learning to walk? Did you beg and plead and ask her a million times a day if she felt like walking? Did you get all freaked out? Did you consult everyone you knew and research the topic endlessly? Probably not. You knew your child should start walking around twelve months, give or take a couple of months on either side. You might have bought a little push toy to help the process. You would have been concerned if she were eighteen months old and not showing any sign of walking. Generally speaking, you probably used your parental intuition and your knowledge of your child to help her learn how to walk.

Ideally, you'll have a similar philosophy toward potty training. One thing I've always found bizarre is that parents assume that potty training is just something the child is going to pick up. Why would they? They might realize it's in their future, but so is driving. The need to pee and poop is a primal one; learning to put it somewhere specific is social, and social behavior must be taught.

I like to remind parents that kids don't know the beauty of potty training. *The only thing they know is the comfort and safety of wearing a diaper,* so getting rid of the diaper is completely uncharted territory. Since coming out of the womb, all they've known is a snug diaper. Some babies have a diaper on before their first feeding! It's like the ultimate security blanket. This is especially important to remember if you're met with resistance. Not wearing a diaper can feel strange, uncomfortable, and unsafe to a small child. It's your job to guide your child through this new territory. After all, using the potty is a skill you've already mastered.

So let's get down to the nitty-gritty. The number one question I'm most asked is, "What's the trick?" Are you ready for the trick? The Big Trick of Potty Training? Memorize this. Study it intently. Are you sure you're ready?

YOU.

Let me repeat that. You, you, you, you, you, you.

YOU are the parent. YOU provide safety and boundaries for your child. YOU are the teacher. YOU provide a loving environment where it's safe to grow. Again, YOU provide the boundaries. It is your job to nurture your child to their fullest potential and instill dignity and self-respect. In the beginning, this process is almost all you. It's going to be up to you to learn your child's patterns and signals and then reflect them back to your child and teach them.

More than just you, it's your *commitment*. This is a big deal, your commitment. Potty training is not rocket science by any means. I can tell you what to do until I'm blue in the face, but until you decide you are committed to the process, it's not going to fly with your child.

When I say "commitment," I mean your commitment to consistency. This is a new skill you are teaching your child. Humans learn by repetition. I repeat: humans learn by repetition.

Even as an adult, have you learned a skill and then not used it consistently and lost it? Of course you have. Pick a skill. I've tried to learn how to knit for years. I start, and then I don't do it enough, and I forget how to do it. And then I have to start with the basics all over again every time. It's ever so slightly easier the next time, but not by much. How about playing a musical instrument? Consistent practice is vital. Very few people make significant progress by playing just once in a while. Think of your job. Skills that are now second nature once took a lot of thought and concentration. After enough repetition, things just sink in.

While potty training, you need to be consistent and firm. By "firm," I mean "without question," not aggressive or pushy. I would say *firm* can be a pretty contentious word in parenting these days. I have so many clients who are afraid of being firm. But being firm and meaning business is *good*, and it doesn't have to look mean. Many parents today are afraid of being an authoritarian presence in their homes. Most of the time, this is because their parents were over-the-top authoritarian, and it left a sour taste in their mouth or resulted in years of therapy. Still, there's a happy medium. Your child needs you to be the authority figure and wants you to be in charge. To have no boundaries is like a free fall through life. So don't be afraid of being assertive and firm—again, not mean, not aggressive or pushy. We'll touch on this throughout the book for clarity. To anyone who is embarking on a new journey, it's never a comfort if the person in charge is wavering.

Consistency is how your child learns effortlessly. How many times did you sing the "ABC" song before your child sang it through alone? Did you sing it a couple of times every couple of weeks and then expect her to sing it for Grandma? I don't know about you, but I think I sang that song twenty times an hour, over and over and over. Remember, too, that *children love consistency*. All children, even adventurous children, love routine. Read it again. Sing it again. Build it again. Things we repeat feel safe to our kids. They know what to expect and are prepared. Spirited children especially need and crave routine.

It's amazing to me that we would expect a child to step up to the task of potty training without this consistency. Examples of inconsistency are to occasionally have them go on the pot but sometimes put on a diaper, or to sometimes demand they go on the pot but other times let it slide. This results in such a constant giving and taking away of responsibility that it's no wonder so many power struggles ensue. Doesn't that make sense? It does to me, and yet I often hear these statements:

"We don't really care right now."
"We're going to wait till she's ready."
"We're just being really casual about it."

"We don't really care right now."

What I think people mean when they say this is that they're not really committed—that it's not a high priority in their lives right now. That's fine. Just be honest with yourself. If it's not a high priority with you, it's not going to be a high priority for your child either. I spend a great deal of time with my clients on this topic. Often parents realize that they are afraid to commit because they don't know what to do and they're concerned that they might fail. More often, though, parents feel something along the lines of, "We just don't feel like it's that important right now," "We are doing other things," or "What's the rush? She'll do it. I mean, she's not going to college in diapers, right?" True, your child is most likely not going to college in diapers. But I routinely get clients who've had to delay preschool and even kindergarten because their child wasn't potty trained. If your child hasn't mastered this task by kindergarten, you probably need some assistance. So, yeah, it might not be vital right at this minute, but it's going to creep up on you faster than you know. And I'll be beating this particular horse until it's good and dead: the longer you wait to potty train, the harder it gets.

Another reason behind the "we don't care" attitude is that something is happening in that parent's life and you know you can't give potty training the attention it needs. That's completely understandable *if* there's actually going to be a break in the action at some point. I remember a mom emailing me. She and her husband were both medical residents, and she was expecting her second child. She felt life was too hectic to potty train. To this, I responded, "It's not going to be any less hectic for your family for a good long time." True, if you are moving or traveling, now might not be the best time to potty train. But if your life itself is busy, you are going to have to carve out some time regardless. If the really pressing reason for not potty training is a delay or special need, I have a whole chapter on that.

This process is going to require attention and focus on your part. Potty training is all you will be thinking about for at least a week or so. However, it will be—it should be—effortless on your child's part.

Do I think it should be a high priority no matter what's happening in your life right now? Yes, absolutely. Here's why:

Environment. One year of one child using disposable diapers uses two full grown trees. Do the math, and it's downright scary. There's no reason to prolong diaper use.

Landfill space. It's estimated that disposable diapers take anywhere from 250 to 500 years to decompose. They are accumulating in our landfills at an alarming rate. What's worse is that very few people dispose of the poop in the toilet before throwing away the diaper (Did you know you're supposed to do that?) so there's the added problem of raw sewage in our landfills.

Your child's dignity. This is one I'll repeat over and over. We both know just how smart your child is. Don't they deserve the dignity of not crapping in a diaper and, still worse, sitting in it? Really think about that. Think about where your child is developmentally and just how undignified this is. I hear parents talk about giving their child self-esteem. Self-esteem comes from mastering a task, from gaining dignity and self-respect. Potty training is a way you can give this to your child.

"We're going to wait till they're ready."

Oh boy. As reasons for delaying potty training go, this is the big one. I'd say this particular rationale is responsible for more potty training drama than any other. If you really follow this thought through, it doesn't make any sense. First, I'll point out some realities of toddlerhood. In what other area of development do you wait until your child is ready? Do you wait until he's ready to go to bed? (I sincerely hope not. That's another book entirely.) How about when your toddler decides they are ready to play with knives? If you have errands to run, do you stay home until your toddler is ready to leave the house? What about if they're not ready to get in their car seat? Do you drive off anyway?

I'm being a bit facetious, of course, but my point is that there are nonnegotiables with our children. We don't let toddlers decide too much on their own; their brains aren't fully formed yet. We are constantly deciding things for them, for their well-being, developmental and emotional growth, and safety. These nonnegotiables exist simply because we, the more experienced humans, understand some things better than our toddlers do.

One of my favorite books in the parenting world is *Simplicity Parenting* by Kim John Payne. The best concept I got from this book is that we are offering our children too many choices, and we are expecting them to have the thought processes of an adult. Children are just beginning to develop their prefrontal cortex. We cannot present them with unlimited choices. If we do, they will not make good long-term choices. To expect them to do so is to rush childhood, which is wild when you think about it. I feel that the idea of "waiting till they are ready" falls into the category of giving the toddler more choices than they can reasonably handle.

In my experience, "waiting till they are ready" leads to disasters. You probably think "ready" is around three years old, as that's become a new societal norm. Not so. That's almost always past ready. Once a child is three, they are well into the process of individualization, when they begin to realize they are their own person and have their own free will and can make their own choices.

This can lead to a drama-filled disaster. It becomes harder to potty train children over three. They have free will and choice and they know how to use it.

So this notion of "waiting till they're ready" is somewhat ludicrous. You are going to have to give potty training some attention and focus, whether you tackle it when your child is two, three, four, five, or six years old. Regardless of the child's age, they will still need your attention, help, and guidance.

There's also the question of what exactly "ready" means. If you are waiting for a magical day when your child up and decides diapers are no longer for him and just does his business on the toilet, you may be waiting a long time. This child is *extremely* rare. And no matter what you've heard about other parents' kids, I have to be honest: I think some parents who say their kid just decided on his own one day have sort of fudged the details. I know this is shocking, but some parents are competitive. Also, I think potty training pains are like labor pains: the details get fuzzy over time.

I'd say my biggest struggle as a potty trainer is this "wait till they are ready" business, because some kids will never be "ready" on their own. We'll get more into what to look for and why many parents miss signs from the child in a bit. Think of diaper wearing as a habit, one they've had since shortly after birth. The longer the habit goes on, the harder it becomes to break.

Dr. T. Berry Brazelton was a renowned pediatrician who became the foremost advocate of late potty training. He promoted late potty training and the whole "wait till they're ready" theory from the 1960s and pretty strenuously at that. It turns out that he was a paid spokesperson for Pampers. Pretty clear conflict of interest, don't you think? Bear in mind that disposable diapers are a $450-billion-a-year business, so there's a pretty high stake in keeping you mucked up about potty training.

Rather than mulling over readiness, I'd like you to think in terms of capability, as in, "Is my child capable of learning this right now?" In expressing this idea to parents, I often use the example of my son learning to tie his shoes. He never really asked me if he could learn this skill, and Velcro had certainly made life easier for parents of young kids. Still, I know that learning to tie shoes generally happens sometime around kindergarten, and I think it's a pretty important life skill. I therefore made a concerted effort, once he hit that age, to buy only shoes with laces. I knew if I bought those with Velcro, I'd cave in to the morning rush. Life will always happen, so if we want to change something, we have to make an effort. I set aside thirty minutes every morning to teach my son to tie his shoes. There was a fair amount of frustration; the worst was on my part for feeling that I was inept or was not being a good teacher despite the fact that I've been tying shoes for years. The whole process required a fair amount of patience from us both. Still, after six days of consistently attending to this task, voilà! My son can tie his own shoes. Did he show signs of readiness? No, not really. Rather, I used an age marker and my "mom sense" to determine that he was *capable*.

In my experience, many not-yet-potty-trained kids are capable and may even show outward signs of readiness. But I think that in our very busy lives, these subtle signs go undetected. I also believe that most people think the desire and willingness to sit and go potty on the toilet will increase with time, as in if they ask to go on the potty once in a while right now, next month they will be asking to go every day. I've found that if you don't seize the appropriate window, the kid just moves on and forgets about it. In other words, the interest in using the toilet does not increase exponentially with time; it peaks and goes away.

Most parents, probably including you, are reading this book because you know deep in your heart that your child is ready. Go with that feeling. I'm going to help you tap into your own intuition about potty training. I'm a big believer in going with your gut.

"We're just being really casual about it."

I hear this one a lot, and to some extent, it's fine. Just know that if you're really casual about potty training, your child will also be really casual about it. By this, I mean you have your child pee in the potty once or twice a day, or you sometimes put a diaper on them and sometimes don't. The problem with this approach is there comes a time when it's no longer appropriate. Maybe your chosen preschool or kindergarten won't allow your child to attend unless they're potty trained. Or you were fine with the casual approach for a two- or three-year-old, but now your child is four, and you feel like it's time to get serious. Stay casual too long, and you will have missed the window of opportunity; consequently, it becomes infinitely harder to train the child. You'll be facing nothing but power struggles, and your life could turn into a living hell.

I also think being casual about it sends a very mixed message. Toddlers are sponges and learn quickly. They are also linear thinkers with no concept of time. So let's say you start with casual potty training. You announce that you are potty training your kid, but what you mean is that you are going to have your child pee when it's convenient, such as in the morning before getting dressed. Or in the evening before their bath. Your child is going to literally learn this: potty training means peeing on the potty *sometimes* but not all the time.

Let's say you take this approach for about a year, which is what usually happens. Then the time comes when the potty training needs to be done already. You say, "Okay, now it's *really* time to potty train." Your child is going to do a toddler version of "WTF? I've got this down. I'm doing what they asked." In switching approaches, you've just added a complicated additional step to the whole process. As a result, you have to reteach the concept of what potty training means.

I think a lot of parents expect that the child will realize naturally that one day, they're going to go pee and poop on the toilet. But in reality, that's a big conceptual leap to expect from a toddler. Why would your child make that assumption when all they've known since birth is a diaper?

The whole casual approach makes me feel really bad for the child. We send one message and then switch it up on them. In fact, the best way to learn something is full immersion.

Most children between eighteen and twenty-four months begin to show an interest in the toilet. Often this has more to do with the toilet itself, the bathroom, and the spinning toilet paper than it does with a bodily function. It's also an interest in mimicking you, the parents. This interest is sometimes all you get as a readiness to potty train, but don't worry if your child isn't showing this interest. I look for other markers as well. This brings us to the next big issue in potty training.

CHAPTER 2

When to Start

Let me state this simply: *when is almost more important than how.*

Unequivocally, potty training is easiest when done between the ages of twenty and thirty months. Bear in mind, these are rough numbers. Sometimes a parent will reach out to me freaked out because their child is thirty-two months and they fear they waited too long. These are just rough numbers; most kids younger than twenty months will have a longer learning curve and need more of your help. However, there also tends to be more agreeableness and fewer power struggles at this age.

Before twenty months is still easier than after thirty months. While I like to use thirty months as a cutoff, more realistically we're looking at a hard cutoff of thirty-six months. Sometime around this age, kids go through the psychological process of individuation. This is the process by which they begin to separate from you. Up until this age, children think they are one with us. If they bonk their head, they think you feel the pain. Around three years old, they begin to realize they are their own person. This is the age of free will and choice and the word *NO!* Anyone with a three-year-old can tell you they are very adept at asserting their will.

It's important to remember that one of the only things your child actually controls is their bodily functions. Layering potty training on top of all this blossoming personality can set you up for major power struggles. It's important to note that three-year-olds rarely need to learn the sensation of going pee and poop. At this age, any struggle with potty training is not about learning but about managing big, emerging personalities.

PLEASE don't fall apart if you've waited past this age. It's still totally doable, of course, but you should know that the learning won't be the focus; finessing the personality will be.

Smack-dab in the middle of that twenty- to thirty-month age range is best for most people. Right around twenty-four months is ideal. At this age, your child is eager to please, is connecting a lot of the dots in the big world around them, is still flexible in their thinking, and is dying for more responsibility. Kids at this age love helping and feeling important. They want to help cook and clean and do chores around the house, so it's the perfect time to hand them their very own responsibility. You want to take advantage of this eager-to-please phase. It's natural and it's good and, unfortunately, it will go away. Trust me.

Mind you, there are always going to be exceptions. More recently, I've seen an increase in moms who know their kids are very capable of potty training before twenty months. And of course, there are plenty of children who potty train just fine in the thirty- to thirty-six-month age range and older.

Why this time frame?

1. There are certain windows of opportunity in development when a developmental task can be accomplished

with the least amount of conscious effort on the part of the child. There are many such windows of opportunity during childhood. We know that learning a second language can be fairly effortless when done before the age of five. The same is true for learning a first language.

2. Since the first edition of this book, more and more parents are choosing to begin potty training between eighteen and twenty-two months. This was actually the expected time to potty train a generation ago. Parents training during this period are having huge success because the potty just becomes another thing the child is learning; it's not wrapped up in any other drama, like the drama of being two. I specifically address kids under twenty months and over thirty-six months in chapter 14.

3. But again, it's not earth-shattering if you've waited longer. This period of time is also a developmental window during which there appears to be almost a lull in learning new skills. Your child has probably learned the basics, like eating, walking, and working through separation anxiety. Now they are just honing their skills.

4. Teaching a child to use the potty imparts them with dignity and self-respect. At this age, your child is learning at the speed of light. You're probably amazed and amused by what they are now capable of. *Capable of.* Do not underestimate what your child is capable of. I see tons of parents gleefully showing

off their child's genius, while that same kid is sitting in their own poop. That's not right. It's insulting to your child's intelligence to think they can't learn this new skill.

5. For several reasons, if you wait too long after thirty-six months, the process of potty training can become a chore for you and your child. At this point, there is little learning to do. I have never met a neurotypical child over three who is clueless about the potty. That means you'll be finessing your child's blossoming personality. If you think you are strong against the will of a three-year-old, you are very wrong. They will beat you every time.

6. Also, as I've mentioned, after thirty-six months your child will be well into the process of individualization, that psychological process in which they learn that they are their own person and are separate and distinct from you. This process, marked by defiance and resistance as they learn to express their free will, is totally normal and to be expected but can create power struggles. In this instance, your child literally holds all the power (their bodily functions). You will not win this power struggle. Trust me.

7. This ideal potty training time frame can usually be accompanied by other markers. These are not definitive. Your child may or may not do these and these markers do not have to be present in order to potty train. They are just some useful gauges.

Does your child retreat to a corner or private place to poop?

Can your child recite the "ABC" song?

Can your child communicate his needs? By this I mean:

- Can your child somehow ask for water, juice, or milk when he's thirsty?
- Can your child somehow ask for a snack when he's hungry?
- Can your child throw a tantrum for candy at the market?
- Can your child throw a tantrum for just about anything?

If your child is retreating to some private place—any place: under the table, another room, maybe even just turning his back—to poop, it is *absolutely* time to start potty training. This means your child is equating pooping with privacy, a natural and correct progression. Your child is showing embarrassment at pooping wherever, whenever the urge strikes. To be clear, these bodily functions are normal, and you should not embarrass your child about them. However, with socialization comes a sense of shame in performing bodily functions in front of others. If we went out for coffee and you pooped in your pants, you'd be embarrassed. I'm warning you: if you don't recognize this sign of readiness and act on it, your child will soon forget to be embarrassed. When this happens, you can end up with a five-year-old who's not bothered at all by pooping in their pants.

In my experience, the "ABC" song is a rough—but by no means definitive—gauge of where your child is developmentally.

Kids who can recite the song have learned some language and most likely learned it through repetition. So maybe your kid isn't bursting out with full paragraphs of speech. If they can say their ABCs, they're probably good to go.

Tantrums are due to your child *wanting* something—anything—and you not giving it. If your child is aware of thirst, hunger, and desires (wants) and can act on those needs, then they are perfectly capable of regulating their bodily functions; your child is ready to be potty trained.

Just in case I haven't beaten you over the head enough with this time frame, I'll reiterate. Between twenty and thirty months is the perfect time to potty train. It's almost freaky how much resistance you will encounter if you attempt to potty train after thirty months. Again, this isn't earth-shattering if you missed it. I'm simply warning you of what might be a struggle.

Now let's say your child has all the markers I've been talking about, and you're just not convinced of their readiness. Or you are wildly unsure. Or you don't want to eff this up. Or everyone is telling you that twenty-four months is too early to potty train. I CANNOT STRESS THIS ENOUGH: if you are attempting to potty train and you have major doubts, it will NOT go well for you. I have seen it time and time and time again. YOU MUST BELIEVE YOU ARE DOING THE RIGHT THING.

You must know that your child is capable of this. It's okay to be a little unsure, but you must be determined. If you are in two camps—sure and unsure—your child will be too. It will look like a hot mess. I tend to use words like *vibe* and *energy*, but really, this is your nonverbal communication. If your mind isn't made up, your child will pick up on it and mirror being sure and unsure.

Whenever I get a client whose situation suggests a lack of determination, I usually start with the "Are you sure you are committed?" speech.

Nonverbal cues can be easier understood if you've ever been around animals, especially dogs. Since we got a dog, I'm a *total* dog person. And since I had a dog and a five-year-old (now much older), I couldn't help but notice many similarities between these two small beings. It didn't take me long to figure out how much information our dog receives from nonverbal cues. This dog knows the different sounds my pots and pans make and which one is most likely to yield a snack. She knows that when my coffee starts brewing, it's time to wake up and pee. But mostly she senses excitement, anticipation, and fear in *me*, and she reacts accordingly.

Once, we were going on a road trip to see my best friend. Stella (the dog) was coming with us, but she didn't seem to get that. That morning, the packing, the anticipation, the energy of going on a trip was driving her bananas. She was underfoot and whining. I finally put her in the car to wait for us, and she settled right down. *She knew something was happening and she wasn't sure what.* Once in the car, she was okay. Like, "I'm going with them. Okay. Cool."

OUR CHILDREN ARE NO DIFFERENT. They are just figuring out the big world around them. They are sensitive and on high alert for new information, largely from nonverbal cues. They are watching, listening, and, more important, *sensing* what it is we are feeling. And they are going to react accordingly.

I think most people don't even realize how sensitive our children are because we talk to them and assume that they understand. So even if we are shaking with fear, we assume that we can talk our way out of it. But with little kids, that's not true. They pick up that vibe way more than they pick up on the words.

I've seen the mere mention of potty training drain the color from a parent's face, send waves of panic through their body, and set off the craziest thread of comments on social media. So many parents jump into the first day of potty training with that same vibe: panic, dread, and fear. And then they can't figure out why their child is resisting or kicking up dirt. Why on earth would a child want to do something that's gotten the grown-up in charge so wound up?

So how do you fix it? How do you stay calm and trust your gut? You think of this as a developmental milestone, not a potential war. You know in your heart when your child is capable of doing this. You don't post on social media when you are ready to start and get sixty-four varying opinions. You realize your child is an individual and will have their own learning curve. You recognize that they may not do this just like your best friend did with her kids. And you realize this is not a measurement of your parenting. It's just something you are teaching your child.

Panic, fear, and dread will only put more difficulties in your path. Relaxed is key.

For now, let's bust some myths and misconceptions that might be blocking your path to easy potty training.

CHAPTER 3

Myths and Misconceptions

So we're clear on when to potty train. Now we'll look at some common myths and misconceptions—some widely held beliefs you may have heard or read about. Some are so common, they've almost become sacred. They've infiltrated day cares, playgrounds, and community centers. Some are convenient sound bites that I often read or hear about. I'm going to deconstruct them here, so we can get logical about all of this. You may need to use some common sense, so be prepared.

Take a moment to think about whether these statements are true or false:

- It's best to wait until your child gives you signals of readiness.
- Boys are harder to train than girls are.
- It's easier to train for pee first, then tackle poop.
- You should put the potty chair out before you start training so your child can get used to it.

Myths

MYTH 1: IT'S BEST TO WAIT UNTIL YOUR CHILD GIVES YOU SIGNALS OF READINESS

False. We've sort of covered the idea of "waiting till they're ready," but let's give it some more thought. What does a parent mean by, "I'm going to wait till he gives me signals that he's ready"? What signals? Some not-yet-potty-trained kids start staying dry during naps or wake up dry in the morning, but that's not the usual case. Some kids show an interest in the toilet, but others don't ever show an interest. Are you waiting for your child to wave a flag that says, "I have to pee"? Remember: all your child has known is a diaper. What signal could they possibly give when they don't know what it is they should be signaling? Think about how you signal for a brand-new action.

Once potty training has begun, your child will have signals. For instance, they might do a pee-pee dance. This could be the classic hopping from foot to foot. Other "dances" or signals could include staying completely still. You might notice that they look antsy or twitchy. Regardless of your individual child's signals that they have to pee, they develop once you've *begun* potty training, not before. To wait for a signal from your child that they are ready to begin potty training is inviting trouble. Since the first edition of this book was published, this idea of "ready" has gone bonkers. I regularly hear from parents with SIX-year-olds, delaying kindergarten because the child is not yet ready to be potty trained. Some kids will never show an inkling of interest or readiness. We still lead them through this milestone.

MYTH 2: BOYS ARE HARDER TO TRAIN THAN GIRLS ARE

Really false. This one ticks me off a lot, mostly because so many people buy this crap. Close your eyes and give this some *serious* thought. Why on earth would this be true? Some people in my classes have suggested it's because girls supposedly mature faster than boys. Perhaps this is true, but it becomes significant much later, like during the preteen years—not so much at two years old. When I see a group of two-year-olds, girls and boys, they all seem on mostly even ground. It's all pretty much "don't hit and please share." If anything, I think boys are *easier* to train than girls because they can pee almost anywhere. He's got to go in the parking lot? Just pull down the pants and pee on the tire.

I've gone down many rabbit holes about this topic and have learned a few things. Female brains are two-thirds the size of male brains (Hold on, Dad, before you start gloating), which means the synapses work faster. Generally, the male brain works in a linear fashion: A to B to C. Generally, the female brain works in a more social fashion; think of a sun with rays or a computer with a thousand tabs open. While this has drastically changed over the past ten years or so, for time immemorial, it was a woman potty training the boys. Most of us women overtalk in many scenarios, while men tend to communicate in clear directives.

I've found potty training boys to be no harder than girls. I refuse to believe that boys as a whole are at this age not as smart or capable as girls.

MYTH 3: IT'S EASIER TO TRAIN FOR PEE FIRST, THEN TACKLE POOP

This is absolutely false. I've heard this before, but I don't even know how you'd approach training this way. This is one of the oddest myths out there, but it *is* out there, so I'm addressing it. Your child will very easily identify both pee and poop as bodily functions that need to go in the pot even though the sensations accompanying them come from two different places. This is not to say that parents and children don't often have a difficult time with poop. Poop actually has its own chapter in this book, and I might point out that it's the longest chapter. It's a big frigging deal that has recently gotten bigger.

For now, just remember that your child has only known squishy poop against their butt. It sounds gross, but it's a sensation they know and are comfortable with. And kids' little bodies generally produce an absurd amount of poop, usually quite effortlessly. The sensation of poop just sliding out and not hanging around is brand-new and somewhat scary.

In general, we are a culture that disdains the very important bodily function of pooping, and that's what our kids learn. Given that, is it any wonder that some kids don't want to poop? Look at how you act about poop, both your own and your child's. You have to make this a very normal, important function for your child. From the time you are done reading this book until you begin potty training, you should be letting your child come with you to pee and poop. It's very important to have your child see that pooping is normal, it doesn't hurt, and its existence doesn't have to be veiled in secrecy. I highly suggest that if you or your partner is a do-the-*New-York-Times*-crossword-puzzle-on-the-can kind of person, get things rolling by bringing your child with you. Have them sit on the floor and read, or you can read to them. Does that sound freaky to you? If it does, it's a good indicator that your poop values are a little more stringent than you thought. Loosen up . . . it will help your child.

All the time, I'll hear parents say something like, "Oh! We are total poop people. Very comfortable with it. Yup. No issues here." And then their kid has a hard time with poop. When I suggest they take their kid with them to poop, they freak out about how weird and gross that is. If this is weird and gross to you, that attitude will be conveyed to your child.

In any event, we'll hit it all in chapter 10, "Poop." Betcha can't wait, huh?

MYTH 4: YOU SHOULD PUT THE POTTY CHAIR OUT BEFORE YOU START TRAINING SO YOUR CHILD CAN GET USED TO IT

I'm sure you've at least heard this, if you're not in fact already doing it. I applaud you for not sneaking up on your child and freaking them out, but please read on with a dash of common sense. The small potty chair was invented to be a less scary version of the big porcelain bowl. The toilet is indeed scary to a little kid. The size is scary, the flushing is overwhelming, and your child's butt is way too small for the seat. So some brilliant person invented a small pot that is just right!

Now I want to ask you a couple of questions. First, look around your house and pay close attention to baby items: high chair, stroller, bouncy chair, talking toys. I'm willing to bet that the small potty chair is the most innocuous piece of plastic in your house. Did you put the high chair out for your child to get used to it? No, you probably put it together and put your child in it and strapped them in. Did you put your child in the high chair "to practice"? No, you probably put them in it to eat and when they were done eating, you probably took them right out. Did you leave your stroller in the middle of the living room so they could get used to it? No, you strapped them in and went for a walk.

Now another question. Would you let your child play around your toilet and bathroom to get used to it? Would you let your child throw things in the toilet? No. It's for one purpose only: pooping and peeing. We usually don't use containers for fecal matter for any other purpose.

Putting a potty chair out for your child to get used to it is useless and counterproductive. If you have already done this, you probably know that the chair has become a basketball net, a stroller, a hat, storage for art supplies, a Matchbox car garage, a step stool, and a doll pool.

Your child does not need to get used to the potty. Putting it out ahead of actual potty training will only serve to lessen its magic. It's for one special purpose and that purpose only.

If you have been doing this, no worries. I'll tell you how to remedy the situation in chapter 5, "Ditch the Diapers! The How-To."

When I start a class, I like to ask everyone where they are in the potty training process. Most often I hear this: "Well, we put the potty chair out so he could get used to it. He sometimes sits on it. Sometimes he asks to go, but not with any regularity. Yesterday he asked to sit on it in the morning, but that was it. When he's naked, he usually sits on it, but when he's dressed, he doesn't usually want to. So, yeah, I guess he's kind of potty trained." Most of these parents report this as success. Sound at all familiar?

"Kind of potty trained" is like "kind of pregnant."

One pee on the pot in the morning is not potty trained. Using the pot while naked, at home, is not potty trained. The sneaky reason most of the parents I've worked with put the pot out for their child to get used to it are really putting it out to see if they will up and decide to potty train themselves. They harbor this secret fantasy that once the potty is out, their child will use it correctly. They haven't yet really committed to the process of potty training.

Once again, using the potty is a skill that must be learned, just like any other skill your child has learned. I'll repeat what I said in chapter 1: children learn by repetition. Therefore, if you put the pot out, you should be ready to teach your child consistently to use it.

I see all kinds of mixed messages and lack of consistency in parents "trying" to potty train. I'll quote Yoda, the wise green guy, for the gratuitous *Star Wars* reference: "Do or do not. There is no try." This goes right along with my theory of "kinda potty training." Or "trying" to potty train. You either are potty training or you are not. Trying does not enter the equation. If you are "trying," you are giving yourself an out.

Are you "trying" to potty train in order to give yourself an out? Why? Convenience? Fear of failing? Not doing it right?

Have confidence in yourself and have faith in your kid. You both can do this quickly, gently, and effectively.

Do or do not. There is no try.

When you are "trying" to potty train, it often looks like this:

31

You ask your child to pee on the potty, yet you turn around and put a diaper on them if it better suits the needs of your day. You ask your child to tell you when they have to pee but ask them to wait a minute while you finish whatever it is you're doing. You put the potty out so they can get used to it, but you don't teach them how to use it consistently. Then the day comes, after months of "trying," when you've had it and get serious. Now you say, "I mean it." But your child has already learned that you don't.

So, no, don't put the potty out for your child to get used to it. Put it out when you mean business: when you are ready to teach your child this new skill.

Common Misconceptions (or, Common Sound Bites)

These are a couple of common misconceptions that I hear in neat little sound bites that warrant enough concern to discuss. They may or may not be on your worry list.

SOUND BITE 1: "BUT I DON'T WANT TO PUSH HIM."

This is probably the second-most-used sound bite in potty training, surpassed only by "wait till they're ready." First, we need to examine where this phrase came from and then look at what it has become in modern parenting.

Not pushing a child to potty train, much like waiting for the child to be ready, started as a reaction to common potty training techniques in the 1940s, when children were strapped down to potty chairs at around nine months of age. They were given soap suppositories to produce poop. They were often abused for accidents or left for hours to sit in their excrement. Just to be clear, *that* is pushing a child. And, yes, it was horrible and abusive.

Then came Dr. Spock and a new wave of thought about child psychology, which introduced the notion that children are actually little humans with the capacity not only to feel pain but to grow up with that pain into maladjusted big humans. The next fifty years gave slow birth to modern parenting philosophies, including the recent rise of attachment parenting (which isn't a new concept at all). And so the pendulum began to swing. I believe that at present, we have swung about as far as possible from the parenting philosophies of the 1940s.

Thanks to rampant social media use and the vicious commentary it often spawns, some modern parenting practices and philosophies have peaked in bitter controversy. Personally, I followed the tenets of the modern incarnation of attachment parenting, mostly during my son's first year. That is to say, I "wore" him in a baby carrier almost constantly, breast-fed on demand, and co-slept. Then I stopped reading books and paying attention to "rules" and started to wing it based on what felt right to me. An excellent resource, which I'm not even sure uses the term *attachment parenting*, is *The Continuum Concept* by Jean Liedloff. The major point I took away from this book is that children should be at the center of everyday life, so they know their place in the world. In this way, they learn that they are one of a whole, be it a family or a community, and they learn about the goings-on in daily life.

Through my work as a potty trainer, I see that things have gotten out of balance in many current parenting trends. In many cases, the child has *become* the center, rather than being *in* the center. The child gets all the focus and often gets a case of terminal specialness. What's also happened is that we have somehow come to think that children can make their own decisions regarding what's best for them over the long term.

You may find yourself bristling against me here, and that's okay. But I want to reiterate the point that every child needs to be nudged to learn new things. We are humans, and we like to be good at what we attempt. Psychologists have found that blindly praising a child can actually limit them into doing only that at which they excel. We don't like to suck at things. As a result, humans—all humans, little and big—will stick to the status quo simply because learning something means temporarily sucking at it.

We parents are responsible for teaching our children and nudging them along in their learning. And check this out: if everything is hunky-dory in your kid's life, what motivation do they have to change? Why would potty training be preferable to diaper wearing? Think about that from the child's perspective. To them, there's no benefit. You are currently doing all the work. They don't need to think or stop what they're doing. You clean up the mess. The status quo is pretty darn good for them, so why change? The nudge to change comes from you because, much like anything that requires learning and practice, we know they'll be better off for it on the other side.

Regardless of your parenting philosophy, I understand not wanting to push your child. However, nudging things along is NOT pushing. Pushing doesn't have to be abusive. Pushing can be you, the parent, following through when your child might not want to. Piano practice and homework are two big things we parents have to push. And you don't have to be all tiger mom about it; we're looking for the pendulum to stop somewhere in the middle.

I remember teaching my son to ski. I had to do a lot of nudging past my son's fear that day because I knew he was capable, and I wasn't going to get off the mountain and go home. I didn't "force" him, but I nudged him. *A lot.* He got frustrated and upset with me, and I got frustrated and upset with him. And we both cried, but I wasn't going to leave the mountain. So I took what I know about him and relaxed about my expectations, and we did it together. And now he loves skiing.

Overcoming these doubts and fears, both your own and your child's, is part of parenting. I could have left the mountain, of course. But my son learned something that day, something that made him shine. Isn't learning something new often filled with fear and doubt? And there's always something amazing on the other side of that. Always.

There's pride in learning something new, in overcoming something we thought we couldn't, for both you and your child. So, yes. Potty training will be your complete focus for the first week or so. But it will be so worth it when you see the look of pride on your child's face that they did something they didn't know how to do last week. Yes, there can be some resistance. The first week of Pascal's kindergarten, about ten kids kicked up so much resistance that you would have sworn torture was on the curriculum. They were actually screaming and kicking. Still, their parents, for various reasons, had to have them in school. And as soon as it became clear that there wasn't another option, the kids settled down and *loved* kindergarten. Once it became the new routine, it was just that: routine. But can you imagine if the parents hadn't "pushed" the issue?

We're going to hit the topic of resistance a bit later in this book, but for now, I don't want you to think any part of potty training is pushing your child to do something they're not capable of doing. No one goes into potty training thinking, *I'm gonna push this to the max. This kid is going to potty train whether they like it or not.* However, I see this happen all the time: parents don't want to push, so if there's any resistance, they go back to diapers. And then they push up against a deadline in which the child MUST be potty trained. They wait until the last minute and put a ton of pressure on the child, and it all implodes. Don't do that. Don't back yourself into a corner, because you'll end up pushing your child in an inappropriate way. It always confounds me at the end of summer when the very parents who didn't want to push their child a tiny bit are now stuck in a powder keg of pressure.

There will come a time when your child HAS to be potty trained, whether for preschool, camp, or kindergarten. Delaying any of these experiences because you were waiting for your child to initiate this process isn't cool. Sometimes we must do some pushing so our kids can develop into awesome bigger kids with bigger-kid experiences.

SOUND BITE 2: "ONCE YOUR CHILD IS POTTY TRAINED, ACCIDENTS WON'T HAPPEN."

I love this one. I see it all the time in social media comments. I see it in blog posts. I hear it on the playground, usually accompanied by some sort of snide attitude: "Not very potty trained if they're having accidents."

Lord help me. When has your child ever learned something and then never made a mistake afterward? Ridiculous, no? To think that your child would never have an accident is weird. I wish there were a magic "potty training switch," and once you turned it on, it would be on forever.

Now, I know that from a logical perspective we all realize this is false. Of course, accidents happen. Still, I find that in reality parents don't really expect them. Most don't prepare for it, and I'd say 90 percent of the parents I see expect *full* potty training in one or two days. You may have an all-star these first few days, but I assure you, accidents can still happen. Potty training is a process. Your child will get better and better at it. This book will get you well on your way. Each week will get easier and easier, and you'll focus less and less on it. Accidents will happen, most often because we—the parents—forget (or ignore) pee-pee dances or don't prompt the child. It's important to remember that accidents are just that; they're not intended. I like to tell parents to be prepared: "Look, you're carrying around a diaper bag right now anyway. What's one more month of carrying around a change of clothes, just in case?"

I like to say that accidents within the first week aren't accidents but learning tools. Both you and your child are still figuring this whole thing out. Of course, something's off if your child is *only* having accidents and is not making it to the potty at all. We'll discuss this later.

True accidents are more likely to happen a few months into the process. This is when knowing how to use the potty has become nothing special. You no longer give verbal praise. You know your child knows their own signals, and you assume they'll tell you if they need to go. That aside, big regressions warrant big scrutiny. Since I brought it up, let's discuss this a little further.

Regression

This problem often arises when parents are expecting another child and fear that initiating potty training with their toddler will end badly, with the child regressing as a newcomer enters the home. Simply defined, regression is moving backward. Children sometimes do regress when a new sibling comes along. Sometimes this is in the form of accidents. Personally, I have never seen a child regress all the way back to pre-potty trained.

Any major transition—a new sibling, a move, a divorce—can trigger regression. The regression is your child's way of acting out their feelings because they're too young to articulate them. Acting out is always for attention. It saddens me when I hear people say, "Oh, she's just doing that for attention." Well then, pay attention.

While regression can be an issue, you should not delay potty training simply because you fear the possibility of a problem. First, you may not have one. Second, with all the work you're going to have with, say, the new baby, you at least want to have laid the potty training groundwork beforehand. Even if your toddler does regress, it is a thousand times easier to get back on track than to start from the beginning.

Also, don't assume your toddler will regress in the form of accidents. Some kids react to a major change in other ways. In the case of a new sibling, they might act out by hitting the new baby, biting you, or ignoring the newcomer entirely. Some kids will have no reaction whatsoever. I definitely advise potty training while you're pregnant and not after the new baby comes. I discuss this in more detail along with some additional tools in chapter 16, "Special Circumstances, including Delays and Neurodiversity."

These are the biggest myths and misconceptions. Most of them, unfortunately, are common and repeated a lot. When you really think them through, though, they have little validity. So now, on to some mental preparation.

CHAPTER 4

Mental Preparation

This chapter is all about getting your head screwed on tight, so it doesn't blow off in preparation for the big day! I know you are champing at the bit for the actual potty training but this is an important part of the how-to (actually, it's an important part of parenting in general). I also want to remind you about the questions and answers near the end of the book. I put the most frequently asked questions there instead of peppered throughout the book, since these questions arise at different points for different people. And based on the number of times people still ask me these questions, I know this section of the book gets overlooked. I'll keep reminding you throughout.

The first thing to do is to get rid of any notion you might have of how long this process should take because this is where so many parents get tripped up. There is an expectation created by too much information on the Internet that potty training should take three days and that if it takes longer, then your child must "not be ready." Yes, it can take a child three days to potty train. It can also take one day. And it can also take seven. I find it interesting that everyone adores the uniqueness of their children and yet many parents want a cookie-cutter version of potty training. There's no such thing. It doesn't exist. I've never seen two children do this the same way. I've also never seen a developmental milestone that brings out so many know-it-alls. I have parents chiming in on my social pages saying, "I potty trained three kids! This is the only way to do it." Yeah. Okay. Three kids, under your parenting roof, doesn't make you an expert. I certainly don't think I know it all even after working with thousands of kids, but I can show you some big trends and have a Mary Poppins bag of tips and tricks.

The biggest problem with having a preconceived notion of how long this will take is that it will put too much pressure on your child. If you allot only three days and then they have to go back to day care, I can almost guarantee that you'll put so much pressure on you and your child that the whole process will implode.

I don't actually have a "method" of potty training. This is more like a guide as to how to approach this milestone and what to do when the literal and figurative shit hits the fan. There are no short-ages of potty training books/courses/opinions. However, there are really only three general ways of going about this:

1. Using rewards
2. Consistency and commitment
3. Using a very casual approach, usually with pull-ups

That's it.

This book is based on the second one. Your child is special. They have their own genetic makeup and their own learning method and speed. We have to honor that. If there were *just one way* to potty train your child—absolutely guaranteed, no hassles, in three days flat—that secret sauce would be viral in nanoseconds. We'd all know about it. But we are dealing with humans who react as in-dividuals and have their own—albeit not exactly logical—thought processes and who not only know how to push your buttons, they actually installed your buttons. Using the potty is both one of the first things you actively teach your child, and one of the first things they actively learn. What you are going to discover through this process is how your child thinks. *Having a preconceived notion of how long this will take is really, honestly going to muck things up for you.* You will unwittingly put too much pressure on your child, and you will drive yourself insane. I know this.

I see people getting tripped up on this all the time. You want to potty train with consistency, and you don't want it to take a year. Realistically, I can tell you it takes most people around seven to ten days. Through all my years of doing this, I've come to believe that there's a truly magical window of about two weeks' duration in each child's life during which they will potty train so effortlessly it's amazing. However, when those two weeks are going to happen for any one kid is anyone's guess, and there's no outward signal as to when they are occurring. So when you hear one of those mirac-ulous stories from your friend/neighbor/sister, they got lucky.

Before you actually begin any potty training, you will need to do a few things in preparation for getting started.

SET A DATE

You need to pick a date to start the process. It can be any start date. You can jump into potty training at any time. To be honest, it's really about you, your mind-set, and the amount of time you can be home with your child. Those are the best predictors for the best outcomes. But life is busy and often gets in the way of the best-laid plans. I used to recommend three or fours days in a row. But over the years, I've learned the hard way that the more days you can string together to be with your child, the easier things will be. Potty training isn't a transferable skill at first. It's best learned at home with parents before moving into other situations. I know this is not always possible and we'll talk about day care in chapter 12. Just do your best. This is why I suggest planning ahead to get the most time to attend to this. This is also to give you a little time to sit with this transition, a major milestone in your little baby becoming a (mostly) autonomous big kid. This can be bittersweet for a lot of parents. We never want to hold our kids back, but it's still a big leap in development.

GET A POTTY CHAIR, OR IF YOU ALREADY HAVE ONE OUT, PUT IT IN HIDING

Every parent who has attended one of my classes has made the "put the pot out so they can get used to it" mistake. If you haven't put it out, don't. If you have and your child has *only* ever used it to pee and poop in, you may leave it out. If the potty chair has been used for anything else besides peeing and pooping, put it away.

I also don't suggest letting your child pick their own potty chair. They'll inevitably pick one with bells and whistles, and you don't need that. This isn't a toy. There are so many brands of potty chairs on the market now that you can pick your price point. My only suggestion is to pick one without a back. A lot of kids need to find different positioning with their pelvis to release poop and the back may prevent them from being able to do so. If your child asks to use the potty chair between now and your selected start date, go ahead and let them. (For more about this situation, see chapter 17, "Random Tips and Questions.")

I am often asked if a potty chair is really necessary. Some parents find it gross, and some parents feel very strongly about the child ONLY using a bathroom right from the get-go. We're not yet into the how-to part of this process, but in the beginning, you will have only seconds from when you or your child recognizes the urge to pee. Travel time to the bathroom may result in pee on the floor.

I also am a fan of little potties because we want to promote independence as soon as possible. If you're going to insist on your child using only the big toilet in the bathroom, you will be part of every pee for a while. A toddler on a step stool, manipulating their own clothing, in a tile and porcelain room, will need supervision for a long while. The little potty makes going on their own much more doable.

CLEAR YOUR SOCIAL CALENDAR FOR A WEEK, STARTING WITH YOUR START DATE

Just to clarify, let's say you've decided to start potty training in two weeks on a Sunday. You will clear your calendar for a week, starting with that Sunday.

This statement strikes fear in every parent I've ever worked with. WHAT?? Stay home? (Don't worry! We'll hit day care situations in chapter 12.)

You will be home for the first few days, with small outings planned. After that, you want to be at your child's bathroom beck and call for at least a week. The reason for this calendar clearing is simple: if you have things planned, you're more likely to get stressed out. What if your child had a lot to drink in the morning and doesn't pee and it's time for music class, story time at the library, a playdate, or whatever? You are more likely to pressure them or get aggravated. You're tempting fate with an accident in the car. What if your child has to poop and you're in the one place that has an out-of-order toilet?

At this point, you will be only three days into potty training, so you have a ways to go before you and your child are absolutely secure in this. Set yourself and your child up for success!

I'm asking you to clear a small amount of time. I've had parents practically flip out and tell me they can't possibly stay home for a few days, to which I respond that if you can't stay home with your child for a few days, you might want to change your priorities. At this age, your child should be neither overscheduled nor overstimulated with entertainment. If you and your partner are both full-time workers out of the home, I've got a whole chapter on day cares; that is its own ball of wax. In a full-time day care situation, it's usually best to pick a three-day holiday weekend and maybe even take an extra day off to make it a four-day weekend. The more time your child has to learn this with *you*, in the familiar setting of *home*, the better it sticks. I can tell you with full assuredness that two days over a weekend will not be enough. An interesting side note to clearing your calendar is that just a generation ago, kids were potty trained at seventeen to twenty-two months. I truly believe it's because the majority of moms were at home. For the most part, they didn't work outside of the home, they had no computer for email and social media, no cell phones, no mommy groups, no playdates, no baby gymnastics, no music classes, and no swimming lessons.

I'm fifty-five, so I know I'm talking about a different generation here, and I'm certainly not saying these moms were better parents. But I do believe it was that stay-at-home factor that made potty training so easy. Between my mom and her three best friends, they had twenty kids in a ten-year span. All four moms used cloth diapers, and none had a dryer. And each of those kids was fully potty trained by twenty-two months. This is absolutely not meant to shame or guilt working parents. It's more to reiterate how important first learning at home is.

If there's any pressure for your child to perform, it'll backfire and have you unnecessarily pulling your hair out. Pressure is the number one killer of the potty training process. Your little one will not respond favorably to it. Do yourself a favor and clear your calendar as best as you can. Please don't make the mistake of assuming your child is going to be the potty training all-star. They exist, but usually where we don't expect them. Do not think I'm making this up. Many parents have fallen prey to the fantasy that "my kid is smart; he'll pick this up. I'm clearing my calendar for three days and then that's it! Back to business as usual. I don't have time for this to take longer than that."

We can't force learning. It will backfire.

Before the Big Day

How to prepare your child really depends on your kid. Some kids do better knowing well in advance that there will be some big changes. Other kids will work themselves up into a lather of anxiety. It depends on your child and what you know about them. I do find it helpful to not keep using the phrase *potty training* beforehand. Kids have heard this term before, and the more you use this phrase without actually doing the phrase, the more anxiety your little one might have.

This is also a great time to start going through the list of big-kid stuff your child does. Kids love hearing about what they can do now that they couldn't do as a baby. This is preparing both you and your child for the end of this baby portion of their life. I know . . . it's so bittersweet.

A word of caution, though: don't overdo the big boy/big girl talk. From the eyes of a toddler, potty training is a pretty raw deal. If you overdo the "don't you want to be a big kid?" talk, it may backfire on you. This particular phase in your child's life is also a place in which your language can generate a mixed message. See if these sound familiar:

"Who's my baby?"
"No, honey, that's not for little kids."
"Stop that now, you're a big girl."

So, what is your child? A big kid, a little kid, or a baby?

It may not seem like that big a deal, but being able to recognize and address this will come in handy. Sometimes our big kids need babying, and it's good when they can separate and articulate that. One child I worked with years ago came up with the phrase "I need some baby love." I thought this was brilliant and adopted it when training my own son. It worked like magic. Kids aren't so afraid of becoming a "big kid" if they know they can have some "baby love" when they need it. Right now, they're in limbo; we know they aren't really big kids, but they aren't babies either. For years, Pascal would ask for "baby love" (actually, he called it mama love, but it means the same). It would last about thirty seconds, and then he'd be onto bigger and better "big boy" things. Still, it gave the two of us that infusion of love and snuggles we both crave. I have found that just noticing certain things your child can do now that they couldn't do when they were babies is cool.

Other than that, I don't think you need to prepare your child. A lot of parents ask me about books, but honestly, I don't think there are really any books out there that actually describe the process even close to accurately. If you're inclined, the episode of *Daniel Tiger's Neighborhood* on potty training seems to be popular. One picture book on potty training will suffice, and that's not even necessary. I have to say, though, I am very partial to *Everyone Poops*, by Taro Gomi.

So you've set a date. You've put the potty chair away for now. You've cleared your social calendar for a week. And you may have planted the idea, supercasual-like, that you are tossing the diapers.

NOW . . . ARE YOU *DONE*, DONE? WITH DIAPERS, I MEAN?
What's the problem? Self-doubt. On the surface, it doesn't appear to be a problem, but in reality, it's the worst kind. It chips away at this process and makes it nearly impossible to potty train. I can always tell when parental self-doubt is the niggling issue underneath a child who "just doesn't seem to be getting it." There are all manner of problems that can arise when you are teaching your child this new skill, but "just not getting it" shouldn't be one of them. If dogs have the capacity to be housebroken in under a week, surely human children can do this as well. If you find yourself saying, or maybe you've already attempted potty training and have said, "He's just not getting it," chances are that self-doubt is your problem.

I call it "*done*, done."

Are you really ready to potty train your child? Are you done with diapers or are you *done*, done with diapers? I know you are going to say you are done with diapers. But are you really?

I find that most parents really can't wait to be done with diapers, but I also find those same parents are in two camps regarding the process of potty training their child: sure and unsure. Where are you? Think about this carefully because it's the best indicator of how the process will go for you. Ask yourself a few questions to help determine where you are.

Are you going into potty training thinking you'll give it a try and see what happens? We've talked a little about the word *try*, but I mean it *for real*: your head *can't* be in this place. "Trying" to potty train sets a clear expectation that you don't expect it to work. Why try? Instead, why not pretend that I single-handedly managed to blow up every disposable diaper factory. (I dream big. Naturally this takes place while I'm clad in a black latex catsuit.) There are no more diapers. Of course, I'm joking . . . kind of. Don't give yourself a wimpy start with, "We're going to try." In fact, if you plan to "try," don't bother starting. It's not going to happen if you try. It will happen when you *do*. Remember Yoda. Do or do not. There is no try.

Are you unsure that your child is ready? Are you worried that they're too young? Most of the first chapters in this book are to reassure you that it is not only possible but preferable to potty train when your child is younger. But if you still think your child is too young or somehow not capable, the process will be an epic failure for you. "Ready" is a nebulous concept. It's better to ask yourself, "Is my child capable of doing this?" Answer this question deep in your gut. Everyone around you is going to have an opinion, I assure you. But *don't listen to everyone else*. Listen to what your heart says about your child.

Why do you want your child to potty train? Be honest with yourself. Yes, pretty much every parent wants to be done with diapers. That's an okay motivator but not a great one. It's like eating a healthy diet to lose weight. You have to have a stronger motivator than that or it crumbles under pressure. Also, look really deep inside. When I first met former client Elizabeth, it was because this whole process had fallen apart for her. She did everything by the book. Also, her child's learning curve was slow. She admitted, in a vulnerable way (which I truly admire), that she was embarrassed. She wanted to be the first of her friends to potty train, and it wasn't going well for her. That wasn't the only reason the process fell apart, but it put a pretty powerful crack in it. Don't potty train right now because you want an all-star. Without fail, you won't have one. Don't do this to prove anyone wrong. What *is* a good reason to potty train your child? Well, to give them self-esteem and self-pride in mastering a skill. My favorite kind of thank-you from parents (and I hear it often) goes something like this: "I just LOVE the look on my daughter's face. She is SO proud of herself." I say it over and over: you don't hand your child self-esteem. They develop it by mastering tasks. *That* is a great motivator!

What do all your friends and immediate family think of you entering potty training? This is *huge*. If every day is a battle for you—all the people in your close circle are jamming down your throat that your kid is too young—you are going to have massive doubts. Potty train anyway, but be sure you get your head on tight beforehand and keep it there during the process. Perhaps don't hang out with any of those people for a week.

I cannot tell you how much a doubting circle of friends and family damages your resolve. I originally tried to potty train Pascal at eighteen months, because I know it's absolutely possible to do at that age. I'm a single mom, and at that time, I owned a store and his day care wasn't on board with my plans. I knew within the first four hours of our first day of potty training that it wasn't clicking easily for him and realized potty training him at that time was possible but that it would take longer than a few days. I abandoned ship, and he did just fine at twenty-two months. The only reason I'm telling you this story is because my circle of "friends" at this time couldn't wait to gloat: "See, told you so." Screw that. For real. I phased them out of my life in short order.

You should be able to potty train your child without everyone coming down on you. "If only I could potty train on a deserted island for two weeks, I'd be fine" is a sentiment I hear often from clients. Don't let the naysayers get you down. I don't know why, but this is an area where people feel very free to tell you exactly what you're doing wrong. It's bizarre to me. Nobody would dream of telling you how to discipline your children.

I think the problem of the naysayers has a deeper level too. If you potty train your kid successfully, then the people who said you couldn't do it look lame. And you've just kicked their parenting advice to the mat. In other words, they have an emotional investment in your failure. So be wary of well-meaning friends who tell you that your child is too young. Or that you are doing it wrong. Or that you should just give your kid a freaking piece of candy every time they poop. Question these folks outright if you're feeling brave: "Why are you so invested in when I potty train my child?"

Plus—I know this from social media—in short order, you are going to have awesome bragging rights. But just don't go into potty training with that as the sole purpose.

If you breezed through those last four questions, go back and ask yourself again. Be sure you are ready to *do* this. Be confident that your child not only has the capability to do it, but that they will blossom in this new skill. Potty train for the right reasons—because it's time, because it's the next developmental milestone, and, yeah, maybe to stick it to Big Diaper. Be sure you have support around you or that you avoid the people who don't support you.

Those points are really important! Yes, it's okay to be a little nervous. Some people have made potty training into a huge ordeal, largely because they waited too long and now have real disasters on their hands. In the majority of cases, though, it's not that big a deal. Sure, it's okay to have a tiny pocket of concern or doubt, but don't go in with the pocket of doubt leading the show. I see this time and time again, and your child absorbs his attitude toward potty training from you. Whether you call it "vibe" or "energy" or "nonverbal cues," the fact of the matter is that children absorb our energy. They feel the emotional undercurrent of any situation. Your child can tell if you are sad even when you're putting on your happy face. Your child is extremely sensitive; all kids are. They don't have the layers of emotional armor we've piled on ourselves so as not to be so vulnerable. *They will feel your vibe.*

If you are doubting, they will be doubting, and the result will look like they're not "getting it." If your prevailing thought is, *I'm not sure they're ready*, it's going to look like they're "not ready" or not "getting it." Expectations, and therefore outcomes, will be unclear. They'll be getting mixed messages from you, and this will confuse them. They won't have the words to say, "Hey, Mom, I'm getting two different things from you right now. I'm not sure what I'm doing here." Instead, it'll look like they just aren't getting it as far as the potty training goes. If your mouth is saying one thing and your heart is saying another, your child will be confused.

Make sense?

Major Issues to Address

Now for a few major issues that need to be addressed. These aren't questions and answers, but addressing these issues is in the "get your head screwed on tight" category.

NIX THE SOCIAL MEDIA POST. FOR NOW.

For the love of all that is holy, *do not post on social media that you are starting potty training*. When you are done, post away. Make a post about it every day for a freaking year if you want! But if you post about *starting* potty training, you will immediately get at least thirty-four comments from all kinds of so-called experts. I'm really glad your best friend used candy to potty train her kid, but *you* know better. Well-meaning friends are going to fill you with doubt. Again, I have no idea why but this milestone brings out all the know-it-alls and it will shake your confidence. So make sure you have a plan, and stick with it.

GET SLEEP UNDER CONTROL FIRST

Yes, we are parents, the legions of the under-rested. I'm talking about you, but more important, I'm talking about your child. Our children as a whole are grossly sleep-deprived. A two-year-old needs around twelve hours of sleep a day, and most don't get anywhere near that much. The craziest thing about sleep is that a tired kid acts like a wired kid. So when it's around seven in the evening and you think your kid isn't tired because they're chasing the dog around in circles, you're likely wrong. That kid is probably overtired.

Another important sign of an overtired kid is if bedtime is a fiasco. Bedtime shouldn't be a hassle. If it is, chances are your child is overtired. Overtired kids are clumsier, have more freak-outs and tantrums, "poke" at others, and are generally fussier. "No I waaaant the pink cup. No. The blue cup. No. The pink cup." You know the drill. Of course, toddlers are known for their fickleness, but tired kids tend to go above and beyond with regard to the crazy.

Fix sleep before beginning potty training. Always, always go for *more* sleep. If you and your child have been struggling with sleep, please get help *before* potty training. My go-to sleep experts are Alanna McGinn of the Good Night Sleep Site and Erica Desper of Be a Confident Parent. They're both amazing at getting parents and children back on track with good, healthy sleep habits. I'm not going to spend a whole lot of time talking about sleep, but you want this duck in the row before you begin.

POTTY TRAIN THE KID YOU HAVE

This is an important one. You have the kid you have, not necessarily the kid you want. You cannot change your zebra's stripes. This is hard for us to admit and hard to remember. We all want the well-behaved, loving, courteous child. But we got what we got. And no matter what, our love is fierce. While you are potty training, be careful not to linger in the "I wish they . . ." fantasy world. Deal with the kid and the problems you have. Your fantasies are irrelevant. Wishing your child would be different doesn't serve anyone. There's a lot of "nature" in this "nurture." While working with a client, I never try to "fix" a perceived weakness. The goal is always to build on what strengths your kid has.

There's another aspect to making sure you're potty training the kid you have. If your child has a particular "problem" before you start potty training—say, they're oppositional or prone to high emotions, you are going to have that same kid and the same problem while you are potty training. That's not a judgment. All of these behaviors are normal, and there's not a single one I have not seen. The behavior isn't the real issue, in fact. The real problem is when parents somehow convince themselves that potty training is going to happen in a bubble, that *all* the other behavior your child typically exhibits is somehow going to disappear while you are potty training. Not only will it still be there, it may even get magnified for a short time. Again, it's all good. Just keep your expectations level.

Remember that behavior is ALWAYS communication. Though we spend our days doing almost everything for our kids, our busy schedules mean that we don't often connect with our kids in the way that they need and want. I'll shamelessly plug my other book, *Oh Crap! I Have a Toddler*, here.

PANTS, CLOTHING, AND INDEPENDENCE

Is your child able to dress themselves? You might want to get started teaching this skill if your child doesn't already possess it. I find it's something we don't even really think about until we start potty training, and then it's like ARGHH!

It's important to remember that a lot of kids don't yet know how to manipulate their clothing. Nothing is more frustrating to you *or* your child than knowing they have to pee and making the move to the pot, only to get tied up in mangled attempts to get their pants down!

A few things can help. First, who the heck started saying, "*Pull* your pants down"? Toddlers are very literal. While teaching them how to use their pants, say, "*Push* your pants down." That's really what they're doing.

Start having your child dress themselves. This, in and of itself, is huge. It gives them such empowerment! It also makes for some massive skill building. When you are teaching your child to dress themselves, it can sometimes require a few more words than "I'm putting your pants on." Remember that this is a brand-new skill to them, so break down what you are doing: "I'm hooking my thumb into the elastic, see? And then I can grab them and push them down."

Some parents have found a "dressing party" has helped. Much like playing dress-up, spend an hour trying on outfits. Make it seem fun! Practice is the key here, and most kids at this age don't get a whole lot of practice. And the pressure of a looming need to pee doesn't make for the best learning either. So set up some teaching time to get the pants down, literally and figuratively. I can't tell you how frustrating it is to be *this* close to consistent peeing in the potty and have the pants mess your child up!

This is also a good time to start really fostering some independence and setting some expectations. Have a set chore for your child, like putting his dish in the sink after dinner. This makes your child feel big and independent, and it envelops them in a feeling of being part of the whole. They *love* having and knowing their place in your home.

SPOUSES AND PARTNERS

This is a doozy!

Be sure your partner is on board with this whole process. This is easier if you get them on board *before* you begin. In my experience, your spouse or partner may not be on board for a couple of reasons, and it's best to sort it out before beginning.

One reason is that when your family is set up with one of the parents working outside the home and the other staying home, the parent who works outside the home has limited time with your child and doesn't want to be the heavy. They just want to enjoy that limited time and have fun. The other reason is that often the parent not on board has opinions and is being railroaded into a major decision and their feelings and ideas are not being considered. I often find this situation to be moms railroading dads, though not always. Many times, moms make decisions about the child without consulting with dad and it makes things wonky.

Some partners really love reading this book and getting involved, and some don't. A good sign your partner isn't on board is if they won't read this book (or at least parts of it).

Many parents I've worked with over the years attempt potty training even when their spouse is adamant about not helping. This never works out. You need help with this process, and your child will most definitely be with your spouse some of the time.

A WORD ABOUT POTTY CHAIRS

I've covered this a bit, but it bears repeating. I not only think it's a good idea to have a little potty chair, I think having a few is even better. We really want to foster independence, but your child most likely is a long way away from being able to manage the big toilet alone, even with a step stool. The potty chair is temporary; soon, they will be big enough for the "regular" toilet. I am a fan of both potty chairs and inserts for the big toilet. I wouldn't worry about any sort of bathroom etiquette at this point. I know some parents feel strongly about only doing poop or pee in the bathroom, but I don't think it matters. Children need the convenience of a close-by potty. Privacy and bathroom etiquette will come naturally with time. I often get some kickback about this from parents who don't want to deal with a little potty. I really, really think you need one, but of course the choice is yours.

POTTY TRAINING A NURSING TODDLER

If you are still nursing, that's awesome. The approach to potty training won't be any different, but there is one twist: because you don't know exactly how much is going in, you have to be a little more alert as to when it comes out. In my observations, breast milk doesn't act like "just" a beverage in the toddler body. It seems to count as food as far as the body is concerned. This means that if your child drinks 10 ounces of water or juice, you can be pretty certain you're going to get at least 6 ounces of pee out at some point. With breast milk, the math is not the same. Do not try to wean your child right before or during potty training! Potty training is a big transition, and your child won't be emotionally able to handle both at the same time. Plus, they may need the stability and comfort of your breast while acclimating to this other big new thing.

PRECIOUS RUGS, FLOORS, OR FURNITURE

Most people I know with toddlers don't have much that's truly precious. If you do have rooms with expensive rugs or items of furniture that cost more than your house, don't potty train in these rooms or make them off-limits for a while. You will freak out when your child pees or poops on these, and there's no greater stall in potty training than a parental freak-out. *Casual* is the key word here. Many parents—mostly renters or wood-floor people—confine their child to the kitchen for a day or just until the child gets the basics down.

POTTY TRAINING IN SOMEONE ELSE'S HOME

Sometimes, because of circumstances, you may be temporarily in a home that's not yours. Maybe you're doing a remodel or maybe having financial hardship. Whatever the situation, you may be living with your parents or in-laws or elsewhere. You should have a realistic conversation with the homeowners. Accidents are bound to happen and if that's going to be a problem, I'd wait to potty train.

REWARDS

Let's take a minute to look at rewards. Episode 30 of the *Oh Crap! Potty Training* podcast goes into fine detail about rewards. Yes, I know many, many people use an M&M or something similar as a reward for peeing and pooping. What you never hear about is what a disaster this can create. The power struggles over the reward eclipse all potty training. I've seen families have to go into therapy because things escalated so much with rewards that it became a different monster and no longer was even remotely about potty training.

I don't think rewarding normal, socialized behavior is necessary. Most of my private clients have tried this, and it's either a mess or they tell me it works about "half the time." Something that works half the time is not working. If you've already started with rewards, the simplest thing is to just stop.

YOU HAVE TRAVEL PLANS CLOSE TO YOUR START DATE

Postpone potty training until you get home. The newly-potty-trained child still requires a lot of focus and energy and, damn, you deserve a relaxing vacation. Even if the trip is a few days after the time frame you're thinking of setting aside for potty training, I still think it's better to move your start date until after you've returned home.

GEAR YOU NEED

There's so much crap out there to buy associated with potty training. I go into great detail on episode 52 of the *Oh Crap! Potty Training* podcast, but suffice it to say that the only thing you really need is a good potty chair (I recommend the original BabyBjörn), a chill attitude, and as much time at home with your child as you can manage. Everything else is cake.

So those are the major issues you have to tackle to get and keep your head screwed on tight. Once you are clear on these points, this process is going to go so much more smoothly! Go back and read the chapter again if you have to. It's worth getting the steps to mental preparation nailed down before proceeding. Once your mind is prepared, take a deep breath, and cue up the music from *Jaws*: dundundundun.

CHAPTER 5

Ditch the Diapers!
The How-To

You've done your mental prep, your head is screwed on tight, you've cleared your calendar, and you are ready to ditch the diapers.

Remember the time line: we are taking your child's awareness from Clueless, to I Peed, to I'm Peeing, to I Have to Go Pee. This time line is potty training in a nutshell. That's it!

(Hahahaha!)

Think of potty training as being made up of blocks of learning. No matter where you are starting from, you need to think of the potty training process as a tower of blocks that you are building. If one block is not learned properly, the tower will be unstable and will tumble. Thinking in this way makes potty training much more approachable. Breaking it down will also give you a good idea of where and when things went wrong if there are any struggles later. Parents who don't break potty training into blocks and have struggles often don't know where it went wrong. With the block approach, you can say something like, "Oh! She had the first block down pat. It was only when we moved to block two that she started struggling." This is extremely helpful for troubleshooting.

Because our kids aren't robots, there are all kinds of emotions, behaviors, and actual gaps in learning that can muck up the final goal. The block method allows us to separate these things out from one another so we can figure out what's causing the problem. As a bonus, potty training doesn't look as overwhelming when we think about it in small chunks.

Here are the major blocks or phases, in order:

1. Peeing and pooping while naked, either with prompting or without
2. Peeing and pooping with clothes on, commando, with prompting or without
3. Peeing and pooping in different situations, with prompting or without
4. Peeing and pooping with underpants, with prompting or without
5. Consistent self-initiation
6. Night and nap (unless you are choosing to get rid of all diapers, all the time, in which case this block is started at the same time as block 1).
7. College: probably still needing to prompt occasionally.

I am going to walk you through each block and tell you how to do it and what you should be looking for. I'll give you some suggestions and a few heads-ups about specific potential problems. (A more complete list of problems is addressed in later chapters.) I don't want to muck up the how-to by discussing every potential problem right up front because many, many parents breeze right through this without a hitch. Ready?

Your Start Date: Block 1

The goal of block 1 is getting pee and poop in the potty with prompting or without. Again: with prompting or without (a lot of parents miss that part). Many books and parents recommend making this day a really big deal. There's one potty training book that suggests a full-out party with balloons and everything. But potty training is socialized behavior. We're not teaching your child HOW to pee and poop. We're teaching them WHERE to put it. We don't create a party for any other milestone or socialized behavior.

We want potty training to be the new norm for your child, and the best way to do that is to normalize the process as much as possible for them. That's why we don't want the potty training start day to be so crazy and out-of-routine that it fills your kid with unease. Childhood anxiety is at an all-time high. My theory is that we're living fast-paced lives in a tumultuous time, and that's rubbing off on our children. So we want the first day to be as chill and as normal as possible.

I suggest you start with little fanfare so that you *normalize* this process as much as is possible. Using the toilet is just something we all do as socialized beings. I remind you here that peeing and pooping are primal behaviors: you don't have to teach your child *how* to pee or poop. Through potty training, you are simply teaching your child *where* to put it. Putting our waste in an appropriate container is *socialized*, and in our particular society, the appropriate container is a toilet.

Here we go! To begin block 1 of learning, take the diaper off your child. If you want, you can make a show of throwing the rest of the diapers away, or you can simply say, "Today, we're not using diapers and you can put your pee and poop in the potty. I'm going to teach you and help you learn this. Yay! It's very fun." You don't have to use those exact words, but you want to state what's happening very clearly and you want to sound like it's cool. Think of how you would say, "Today we're going to the dentist," and try to hit the same tone. You want to sound cool and casual, and avoid any hint that you anticipate drama. Clear. Succinct. Direct. Don't ask their opinion about this. *Don't ask, "Okay?"* In fact, don't *ask* anything. We don't want to give them the opportunity to say no.

You will be home all day today. Your child will be bare-bummed *all day*. This can be naked or just bottomless but it's vital that they have zero clothing over their butts. Much of the day is going to consist of you catching your child as they're beginning to pee and getting them to the potty. If there is any covering on their bum, by the time you see the pee, it will be too late: their bladder will have emptied. The other benefit to keeping your child naked today is that you will be more likely to see their pee signals. Almost every kid gives some sort of signal right before they pee. It may be subtle, so be on the lookout.

Another common question about naked/bare-bummed is this: "It's really cold where we are. Does he HAVE to be bare-bummed?" Yes. The answer is yes. Either jack up your heat or wait until summer.

Throughout these blocks, I often say, "Get them to the potty." For some kids, picking them up to rush them to the potty results in either resistance or going stiff as a board. In these cases, it's totally cool to bring the potty to the child. Actually, it's totally cool to do this in all cases.

I used to suggest extra fluids on this first day, but over the years, I've come to the conclusion that it's best to get a handle on your child's normal drinking and peeing schedule. This is especially true if you have limited time at home and your little one will be heading back to day care or preschool.

I will warn you that this is going to be the most exhausting day of your life. I have two reigning philosophies: (1) we always leave room for the miracle and (2) I will never sugarcoat a truth into a lie to make you feel better. Yes, this day may go more amazingly well than your wildest dreams. It may also make you want to poke your eyes out with a fork. Your job today is to *do nothing but watch your child*. If this sounds unbearable, remember the pot of gold at the end of the rainbow! Still, I cannot stress this enough: TODAY YOU WILL DO NOTHING BUT WATCH YOUR CHILD!

Have fun projects planned. Play trains and dolls and puzzles. Watch videos, read stories, dance around naked. Let the dishes go, don't vacuum or dust, don't do laundry. You will be on your child like white on rice. No computer! Don't get on the phone! Don't read a magazine or book!

Many parents tell me it went wrong from the first day. "She just peed on the floor." I'll go through the day with them and learn that Mom or Dad just "had to" get on the phone because of this, that, or the other thing or "had to" check their email. You can't do that; you have to watch your child and help them get to the potty. At this stage, your child is not yet able to pick up on their need to pee without your help. If there is some pressing matter in your life—someone's in the hospital, you're on call, anything that will pull your attention from your child—*then don't pick this day to potty train*! Most often, it's the moment you turn your back that your child will pee on the floor.

One way to make this exhausting day sound easier is to think of it as a great bonding opportunity. For me personally, after the first day of potty training, I felt closer to my son than I had in months. Around twenty-four months, our kids start showing some independence, and we're thrilled! For the first time since birth, we can maybe sit for a moment with a cup of coffee and read an article. We very rarely watch every move our child makes. The house has been child-proofed, they can walk without killing themselves, and we get a breather. Think of this day as a special opportunity to reconnect. I remember being surprised: there were all these little things he would do that I hadn't seen. Also, I figured out what was happening to all the damn Legos (stacked way under the couch cushions. Who knew he had a secret stash?).

One mom reported to me, "We had SUCH a blast that first day! It was almost decadent to get to stay home and just focus on him all day and not rush around doing things. We played all kinds of games, it was just so fun, and he did so great. I was so impressed with him!" What I really loved about this mom was how impressed she was by her son, though the way I see things, it took both of them working together to make that first day of potty training successful.

Let's break this day down starting with that first pee. If you're doing your job, *which is watching your child*, you'll catch that pee quickly. Don't panic, don't scream. Just say something like, "Oo, oo, hold it, honey . . ." Pick your child up and get them to the potty ASAP. The hope is that you'll make it in time for some of the pee to go in the pot. Yes, you will possibly leave a trail of pee behind;

this is why it's vital to keep the little potty close by. Don't make the rush to the pot frantic or scary—just quick. Once the pee is in the pot, you have lots of options, depending on your child. You can high-five, fist bump, have them look at it and empty the potty into the big toilet, or just say, "Thank you" or "Wow. You did it." Many parents get so excited, they go full blast with excitement. OMG! YAY! I'M SO PROUD OF YOU! All caps because they're yelling. This exuberance can backfire on you. It can freak out your little one, but it can also trigger some perfectionistic tendencies, especially if your child is already prone to being a perfectionist.

You are not to ask your child if she has to go. Never, in the coming week, will you ask your child if they have to go. (This confuses some parents.) You will instead prompt them using a statement, a choice, or a challenge—for example:

1. A statement: "Come, it's time to pee." Or: "Let's go pee."
2. A choice: "Would you like the big potty or the little potty?" Or: "I have to pee. Do you want to go first or second?"
3. A challenge (great for spirited or oppositional kids): "I bet you can't fill that potty with pee." Or: "I bet I can beat you to the potty!"

Just don't ask the question, "Do you have to go?"; you'll likely get a big no.

So, back to that first pee. I've seen greater success from parents who wait for the first pee to start and then run the kid to the pot than from parents who randomly sit the kid on the pot to try to pee. Do you see the difference? Some people maintain that if you just put your child on the pot every half-hour or so, eventually they'll pee. A lot of day cares train this way, and it tends to work great in a group setting, when everyone goes to the potty. But at home, I've found it's more effective to wait for the child to start peeing and then get them to the toilet. I think this is because they make the connection between "feeling" and "doing" faster this way. Just sitting on the potty and waiting for the pee doesn't allow them to connect the dots as quickly. I also think it's super annoying. Can you imagine someone making you sit when you don't necessarily have to go?

Over the course of the next few pees, one of two things will happen: either your child won't recognize that they're peeing (still clueless), or your child will notice that they've peed or are peeing. Most kids skip directly to the "I'm peeing" stage, which is typically characterized by a funny look on their face. This look is part interest—there's a certain fascination in watching yourself pee, to be sure—but they'll also probably look at you like a deer in headlights: "Uh-oh . . . what am I supposed to do now?" Keep an eye out for this look. Often it comes right before the pee, and it can help you get your child to the toilet in time.

By the third pee on this first day, they'll probably know it's coming one to two seconds before it actually starts. Rush to the potty. Every time they pee, they'll know a little further in advance, which will buy you a bit more time to get them to the potty. Watching your child closely this first day will also give you an idea of what kind of pee-er you have. Some kids do five little pees after taking in some fluid; others wait an hour and then do one huge pee. This is what I call their *pee pattern*. Learning this is going to give you the information you need to get back to daily living. It also gives you information to relay to other caregivers or day care: "She usually has a big pee around eleven o'clock" or, "He can go hours without peeing, but once he pees, he does like five pees within an hour, so be on the lookout."

Being naked, your child may very quickly catch on and sit by themselves. A quick note about boys: definitely have him sit down to pee for now. Hold his penis down for him, and put his knees together to hold it down, and tell him what you're doing to teach him how. I often get asked how to teach this, and it's literally what I just wrote. Consistently, tuck the penis down, put his knees together, and release the pee. Many parents buck against this because the child wants to pee like daddy. For the newly potty trained, this usually ends up a disaster. It's a loaded fire hose and will be used as such. Also, they can't stand and pee in the little potty chair because it will splash right back. And they will need help to use a step stool on the big toilet, making them dependent on you for every pee. Of note: I've never seen the splash guard on the little potty work when sitting down, so don't rely on that either.

Somewhere in block 1, you should start to get good at noticing "that look" in your child's eyes, which is generally accompanied by some sort of physical signal that you'll begin to recognize. You may see them standing perfectly still or stop playing. They may or may not signal with their hands or words. When you see the look or signal, help them get to the potty. This is what I call their signal or their *pee dance*. These first few days of potty training, this is what you, as the parent, are learning: their pee pattern and their pee dance. Sometimes you may not see any signal. In that case, you will be a bit more reliant on the pee pattern.

Even if your child is a camel, though, remember: no *asking* if they have to go. You are looking for that pee dance before prompting (remember to prompt with a statement, a choice, or a challenge). Expect success. You may even be getting a few seconds of heads-up that the pee is coming.

The first several pees may not go in the exact order described here. It may take your child a few pees before you get that extra second or so of warning. Just remember that the general idea is to increase your child's awareness to the point that they can tell you before they have to go. To help build that awareness, it's a good idea to reflect their signal back to them. "Oh, look, you're walking on tippy-toes. I think that means some pee is coming. Let's go to the potty." Or, "Hey, you're grabbing your crotch. That means it's time for a pee. Do you want to use the big potty or the little potty?"

Offering a choice here can be KEY. This works in general parenting as well. Be cautious though: it should always be a choice between only two things, and those two things should be something you approve of.

If you're not seeing this progression of awareness, it's okay. It's hard to determine how well things are going in these first few days. It's also common to have what looks like a disaster in the first two or three days and then have things magically click into place.

I cannot state this enough: potty training is an individual learning curve. You cannot compare your child to any other child you know. The societal expectation of potty training in three days flat is bullshit. Give your child time to learn this skill. I don't like to judge the process at all until you've given it a solid seven days.

Still, if you're worried that there is no progress, it's worth taking a minute to check in with yourself. Are you truly watching your child, or have you gotten distracted? Are you making too big a deal of all this? There is a delicate balance between prompting and backing off. Remember that potty training should be an effort for you but *not* for your child. Are you hounding them? In your child's mind, today should be about special one-on-one time with Mom and/or Dad and learning a new skill.

Don't let drama and your nervousness take over. Children resist when there's too much pressure. As with parenting in general, if you are met with resistance in potty training, you must examine your own actions. Sometimes we don't realize the pressure we're putting on our kids. Remember, pressure can be verbal or nonverbal, and kids are masters at picking up your nonverbal cues. Maintaining focus on your child while not putting too much pressure is hard. It's a balancing act. A helpful tip is having stuffed animals or dolls "demonstrate." You can also line up a little audience of these toys and have your child show them how it's done. But on that note, combined with too much pressure, is this: don't make every single thing about the potty. It will wear your child out. Some parents go overboard with books, videos, constantly mentioning potty training, let's video-call Grandma and Auntie and tell them. Remember: as excited as you might be about the pee in the potty, we want to make this as normal as possible as quickly as possible.

Few kids go straight from this first day of potty training into telling you with words that they have to pee or poop. This is important to remember. A lot of parents expect that the verbal indication will happen sooner than it does and are befuddled by the number of accidents their child has. From start date to self-initiation usually takes about three to six weeks for most kids, even superverbal communicators. I'll repeat this since it's often missed. Self-initiation (their asking or telling you directly that they have to go) usually comes about three to six weeks into the process. Even if your child does start to tell you on that first or second day, it's usually not with consistency, so don't completely back off and leave it up to them.

As for that first poop, remember how weird it is going to feel to your child, who is used to pooping in a diaper. My advice, as with pee, is to wait for it to come rather than using the "sitting and trying" routine. Signals of an impending poop to watch for are an intense look of concentration, grunting, twitching, indicating physical discomfort, rubbing the belly, sudden crankiness, and retreating to a corner, under the table, or some other private place. You then put your child on the pot. I really do suggest the little pot; the squat used to sit down will help ease the poop out. Have wipes or toilet paper handy, grab a favorite book or two, and get comfortable. Read the stories to your child. If they grunt and screw up their face, just softly offer encouragement (I say softly because this is sort of an inward function). "It's coming, you can do it. Uhh. Go ahead, honey, let it slide out."

Encourage but don't pressure. If your child gets freaked out and starts to cry, you can give them a hug while they're on the potty. For the first few poops—and most kids will go down to pooping once a day—you may have to read to them for a while. That's normal. It is normal to not get a poop on that first day. Many kids have a sort of performance anxiety about it. Don't sweat it if there's no poop. However, think about why no poop was happening. Maybe it looks like they didn't have any poop or they needed to poop but couldn't. There are many, many things that can go sideways with pooping. We'll talk about all those things in chapter 10, "Poop."

But let's assume everything is great and your little one dropped a hot one in the potty. Most kids love looking at their poop and dumping it in the big potty. This is the reward: you get to flush your own poop. Be aware, however, that some kids are repulsed by it, and be ready to pivot if that's your child. There's no reason they need to look at and dump it if they don't want to.

Praise

I know this is super exciting, especially when it's going well. Simple, direct praise is fine (don't go overboard), but I also really recommend *reflection*: we simply reflect what happened instead of the ubiquitous "good job" or, worse, shrieking, high-pitched praise. Reflection sounds something like this: "That was a giant poop!" or "Wow, your belly must feel GOOD after pooping like that!" I've found that kids respond well to adjectives and exclamations like, "huge," "tons," "wow," and "my goodness." I've also found a simple fist bump with a quick "awesome" or "you must be proud of yourself" to suffice.

In recent years, many articles have been published about the perils of excessive praise. One thought is that it can make a child connect only with a desired outcome, not with the effort needed to achieve that outcome. The concern is that this leads children to give up when something is hard and/or only fosters self-esteem through achievement.

However, reflection is a really good tool to use in all areas of parenting. It acknowledges the effect and the outcome without attaching judgment to it. What I've seen in potty training is that excessive praise can backfire because the child can become obsessed with doing it "right." And that can really go sideways. I also think a small amount of praise is fine because there really is only one desirable outcome here. Just don't go overboard.

On that note, be aware that words are powerful. Be cautious not to continually say "It's okay" when your child has a pee mishap. Better to reflect and say something like, "Oh, you peed on the floor. Next time, I know you'll get it in the potty." Remember that these first few days are data collections; these aren't accidents per se, as they're still learning. But when you use the literal words "It's okay," your child could very well interpret that as *It's totally okay for me to pee on the floor.*

Poop

Poop is a huge deal. HUGE. So huge, it's got its own chapter. For now, though, let's just address the single biggest poop question I get: what to do if you missed the poop or your child didn't poop at all on the first day of potty training.

Most kids show some sort of sign that they are about to poop, but some can drop it like it's hot. If you miss the poop that first day, it's okay; the whole process doesn't fall apart. Get back on the horse. Don't let it undermine your confidence. Clean it up and say something simple and to the point. This is where reflecting back to the child is really helpful: "You pooped on the floor. Poop goes in the potty. Sit on the potty to poop." Simple and direct. You don't want to scold your child on this first day, but it's very important that you communicate in tone, voice, and body language what you expect. This concept is brand-new, and your child needs to learn the rules of the game. Again, don't say "It's okay" if poop ends up on the floor. For some kids, those specific words imply permission.

If your child doesn't poop at all on this first day, or if they normally poop in the morning and don't today, it's not a big deal.

Again, we'll be looking at poop very closely soon enough. Pooping behavior generally changes during potty training. When wearing a diaper, most children poop as many as three or more times a day. During potty training, that typically goes down to about one poop a day. I suspect it's a natural consolidation and part of socialization.

Anyway, if your child doesn't poop (or doesn't poop at the normal time) today, it's nothing to be concerned with. As for holding poop, yes, it can be uncomfortable, but most children can go longer than you would think without a poop before most pediatricians will even blink. Your child is in no danger if they don't poop for a day or two. I want to remind you again that your vibe is running the show. If you are freaked out or overly anxious about getting a poop out of your child, that may put your child on high alert, and poop doesn't often release when the body is on high alert. The best thing to do is to act supercasual, keep calm, keep your vocal pitch low and soft, and assume the poop is (eventually) coming.

And a repetitive note about "accidents" in block 1: any pee or poop that ends up on the floor is not an accident at this point; it's a learning tool. Have your child help clean up and don't scold them. Use positive but simple language. "You are learning. You pooped on the floor. Next time, your poop goes in the potty."

So now it's nap time on day 1. If you aren't simultaneously doing nap or night training (I fully run through this in chapter 6 on night training), you will now clearly and directly tell your child what is going on: "I'm going to put a diaper on you for nap time because you're still learning. You've done such a good job today, and your nap is a long time. You may not remember to pee when you're sleeping. When you wake up, we're going to take it right off."

You've stated it clearly so your child knows what to expect and why. No child I have ever worked with has ever questioned this. It's like they know they'll be asleep and not in control of things. I've also never had a child bring up the fact that just four hours ago you made a big deal of throwing out said diapers. I would also make sure to have a go at a pee before a nap.

I used to suggest holding off on the nap if you hadn't gotten a poop in the morning hours. This is ultimately your call: you know your child's routine best. If you suspect a poop is brewing, you can slightly delay the nap, but I've come to the conclusion that having a tired child is the quickest way to derail potty training, so don't hold off on the nap for too long. You need your child rested. If they do poop in the naptime diaper, it's okay for the moment. If it becomes a habit, you will have to deal with it. Typically the child isn't holding the poop in specifically for the nap diaper. Rather, there's been a lot to learn, and as they relax during sleep, the poop just comes naturally. You should dispose of the poopy diaper as you normally would. I do not suggest you let your child dump the contents of their diaper in the toilet. The entire process of potty training is teaching your child that bodily functions go in the toilet. For them to do it in their diaper and then dump that is not the connection we are looking for your child to make.

After their nap, continue on with the day the way it's been.

I wouldn't put any sort of thought into whether the nap or bedtime diapers are wet or dry. If your child has shown progress during the day, a wet diaper means nothing. As your child gets better at holding it until they reach the pot, they may naturally start staying dry. Also, in the beginning phases of potty training, they may not yet be fully emptying their bladder, so nap and night diapers may be fuller than usual. This evens out with time and practice.

If you intend to give up all diapers, even for naps and night-time, be sure to read chapter 6, "Nighttime Training." It's actually a better way to potty train, but I understand that it can look over-whelming to attempt.

You will likely be exhausted. Your child will likely be exhausted. This is big learning. This is the first time you've had to teach some-thing in a specific order, with only one desirable outcome—and in a relatively short time. There's a lot more going on here than just pee and poop in the potty. This is a huge boost in autonomy and I've heard many times that language takes off after potty training. I also have full confidence that you and your little one can absolutely do this. But yes, it's totally exhausting. Your kid has had to learn a lot about something they paid no attention to until a short while ago. Many children may seem more needy or clingy. If you are still nursing, your child will probably want to nurse more. This is all okay too and expected.

Chances are this first day has left you either elated or bummed. You may be stoked that you and your child both have a good han-dle on this potty training thing, or maybe you think your child absolutely didn't get it. If it seems to you that this first day didn't prove so successful, examine where and when things might have gotten tripped up. Check in and be honest with yourself on what you may have done to hamper the process. I encourage you to look at your own behavior during potty training rather than putting it solely on your child. Many parents have told me that their child is too intense, too stubborn, or too something, but—and I say this without judgment—usually these parents tend to be the same. So not only have the parents passed this trait on to their child, but they (the parents) act this way during the process of potty training. Know your own style, and be willing to adjust accordingly. Try to strike the careful balance of being extremely attentive without being overreactive or overbearing.

At this point I also feel it's worth mentioning a particular phenomenon I see as a mom and as a potty trainer. Parenting has gotten oddly competitive in a strange way. Most of us know it's not healthy to push our children to see who can read sooner and who can spell or do whatever else better. Still, there's an odd thing happening that I don't even think most parents are aware of, which is a sort of reverse competitiveness. It's as though parents are competing to have the child who is most special because of a negative: he refuses sleep, she's always sick, he's so intense, she's never done what everyone else does, he never lets me eat, and so on. Please don't make your child special for not potty training. It's an area where it's just fine to be average.

In any event, should you feel your child really hasn't gotten the gist of potty training after the first day, that's okay. Our twenty-four-hour system dictates that you move on to day 2, but it's totally fine if you're still in block 1 as far as learning goes. **The blocks are defined by progress made, not by time passed**; you may still be on block 1 on day 2. I can't state this enough: *every child is different*. Remember that time line we talked about? Clueless, to I Peed, to I'm Peeing, to I Have to Go Pee? Look for progress, not perfection. Nothing is really a problem on these first few days. It's vital to remember how new this is to your child. We cannot expect them to get it just because we say it. This whole thing is a process. If they need a little more time on block 1, that's fine.

As soon as you get a sense of hope or that a light bulb has lit up in your child's head, it's time to move on to clothes. You don't want to stay on block 1 too long. That can result in an "only potty trained when naked" kid, and unless you live in a nudist colony, that's not really potty trained. Again, block 1 doesn't have to be absolutely perfect. Move on when you have an overall sense of progress.

We are paying more attention to blocks than days here, BUT, but, but . . . most often the second day of potty training, whatever block of learning you are on, can bring resistance. We will discuss this in chapters 7 ("Block 1 Drama") and 8 ("Block 2 and 3 Dilemmas") more fully, but I offer a heads-up early on. By day 2, the fun is gone, you are serious about full-time potty use, and your child is over it . . . and may crank up the resistance. Expect it. It's normal, and we'll bust through it when it happens.

> End result: If your child, while naked, can sit to pee and poop on the potty, this would be a successful completion of block 1. This can be because you prompted, you led them, or they went on their own. *If you do not see this, you are still on block 1 and should not move on until you see a successful completion of the end result.* Don't expect perfection, but you should have a sense of your child starting to get it. The biggest indicator of getting it is how *you* feel. You may be tired, yes, but you should feel hopeful. If you are disappointed or feel like crying, your child simply needs more time on block 1, and that's fine. *Block 1 normally takes anywhere from one to three days.*

Block 2

This block still requires your watchful eye. I cannot state this enough: block 2 isn't necessarily day 2 of potty training. What we are most looking for is to get your child in clothes. Both you and your child should have a sense of when the pee is happening when you start this block. Again, it's not likely going to be in words or self-initiation. Whether with a look or a pee-pee dance, it should look like a light bulb of sorts is going off in your child's head, even if they indicate it by crying or noticing if they don't make it to the potty. That recognition is good!

COMMANDO

Your child should go commando (no underpants but with pants) for about a month, give or take a week. I used to merely suggest this, but over the years I've learned that it is a necessary step. Underpants are too much like a diaper. A few days of potty training is not long enough to reprogram your child's muscle memory. That muscle memory dictates that when something snug around the waist and upper thighs goes on, it's time to release the pee and poop. Because this is largely unconscious, it's beyond your child's scope to control it. In other words, they can't be expected to do anything *but* poop and pee in the underpants. I've had many people laugh this idea of muscle memory off, which is totally fine. Feel free to try underpants if you want, but if your child pees or poops in them first thing, take them off.

Because they fit snugly, underpants somewhat contain an accident, particularly a poop. This may seem advantageous, but it's not; I've seen kids have accidents in underpants and not be too bothered by it. However, because going commando feels similar to being naked, an accident in pants with no underpants feels much different. To be honest, it feels much grosser. The pee trickles down their legs, and their pants get all stuck to them. That's good in potty training. Kids seem to have a sense of embarrassment when an accident happens while going commando that they don't really feel during an accident with underpants. I think this may be because kids see underpants as a diaper in another form. When I say a sense of embarrassment or shame, I'm not suggesting that you shame your child; I don't advocate that at all. There is, however, a natural sense of shame that develops during the process of socialization, and an internal sense of this is an indication that socialization is occurring appropriately. Think about yourself or anyone over potty training age. Pooping in your pants would definitely embarrass you, even though it happens to just about all humans at some point. That's because it's socialized behavior. Any child can go without underpants under shorts or pants, and no undies under a dress is perfect.

Another possible reason that kids seem to have more accidents early in potty training if they're wearing undies is that underpants afford a certain level of privacy. If the genitals are all tucked away nicely, it seems to the child as though you can't see them having an accident.

As for cleanliness, going commando is fine hygienically. I have had parents who are worried about this, but underpants are a layer of fabric—nothing else. At this age, I can guarantee you are washing their pants or shorts every day. Going without underpants is not a big deal and can save you lots of frustration. I have never seen or heard of a child developing any sort of infection by not wearing underwear. I would stay away from pants or shorts with a stiff seam in the crotch, which can be irritating. Day cares and commando are another ball of crappy wax entirely. You may have to rush this step in order to get back to day care but I'll address that in chapter 12, "Day Care Struggles."

WHAT'S THE DEAL WITH TRAINING PANTS?

Training pants are underwear with a triple layer of cloth in the crotch. They went out of fashion for a couple of decades when the Big Diaper companies showed their claws with pull-ups. Training pants are useful *when it's time to move to underpants* because they are a version of underpants.

I quote a client: "To all you moms out there, when Jamie tells you to do things a certain way, it's based on a lot of experience, so you should listen to her! I tried the training pants again on day five when we visited my mom. Six accidents in four hours! The next day, back to commando, & either no or one small pee accident. She's doing so great now!"

If you're still digging in your heels about commando, go ahead: try underpants if commando totally weirds you out. But if your child starts having accidents, you should immediately ditch them. Accidents in pants turn into a new habit faster than you can blink your eyes.

UNDERPANTS

After a few weeks or so, your child should be able to start using underpants without any problems. If you have tempted your child with fancy character underpants or if your child knows about underpants, you should hide them for now to avoid any fights about it. If your child *begs* for undies, you can give them a go. Some kids have a super-high integrity about not peeing in their underpants, especially if you've chosen character undies. If it works for you, go for it. If not, be willing to ditch them fast.

I'm going to say it one more time because this is one of the most asked questions on social media: "But can't I just try underwear right away?" The answer is do what you want, but do not come back to me telling me how potty training didn't work.

Also worth noting: you'll be ditching onesies, overalls, footie pajamas, and pants or shorts with complicated buttons and snaps. It seems obvious, but I find it often slips parents' minds. I highly suggest elastic waistbands, at least for a while. Your child is still going to give you only a five- to ten-second heads-up, so you need to be quick about getting the pants down. Plus, you want to make it easy for your child to do it themselves if they want to. If your child is hindered by their clothes and can't make it to the potty in time to pee, chances are they will feel embarrassed and have a meltdown. Set yourself and your child up for nothing but success.

One more note about underpants, commando, and the whole shebang: *pull-ups are diapers, plain and simple.* I have no use for them. They prolong potty training indefinitely. No child uses pull-ups as underpants, and if underpants feel too much like a diaper, what do pull-ups feel like? A diaper. Don't waste your time or money. Great marketing has led us to believe that you can potty train your child while in diapers. But that sends the child a huge mixed message and extends potty training by months. I highly suggest you don't do this.

CLOTHES

Block 2 brings clothes. And I will make no bones about it: block 2, which usually comes around two to six days from your start date, is *the hardest phase*. This is when most people quit potty training and most parents panic. Naked (block 1) goes well, but then clothes muck it all up. Keep going. It will click.

It is normal for your child to wet their pants at first. They may wet all the way through the pants. Don't be devastated. Have them help you get a new pair of pants and clean up. This is common, but I regularly have moms contacting me who are practically in tears that their child is not getting it. We have got to give them a minute to learn this. Typically, putting pants on, commando, is in the very beginning of potty training. They need a minute to catch up. Kids do not and cannot just up and do something new because we ask them to. For all we know, they're processing the information and at any moment will discover the right order of things.

If you have decided to do night and nap together, you obviously won't be using diapers; otherwise you will still be using diapers for naps and bedtime during this block.

You may find that occasionally, upon prompting your child to use the potty, you will be met with a clear, firm "No." This is different from resistance (which looks more like trying to put a cat in a bucket of water). What I'm talking about here is a simple "No," and when you hear this from your child, you need to respect one of two things.

First, *they may not actually have to go (which doesn't mean they won't have to in a few minutes)*. By the end of these first few days, you should have a handle on your child's patterns and will pretty much know with at least some warning when they have to pee. I say this because, again, you want to avoid hounding them or over-prompting. You want to have at least a rough idea of when they may have to go so you're met with success. When a child says clearly that they don't have to go, respect that. A phrase I suggest is, "Okay. I trust you to come tell me when you do. I'll be in the kitchen when you need me." Period. Notice I said "when," not "if," implying that this *is* going to happen; it's just a matter of time (a subtle shift in language). Don't belabor the point. Just tell them where you'll be, which is important because in the beginning phases of training, they can't hold it long enough to search for you around the house. Another tactic is to say, "Well, let's try. If nothing comes out, we can try again later." A third tactic is to agree with them but set a timer. Here's the trick: offer them a choice of times, making the times small, "Okay. I'll set a timer. Do you want to go in six minutes or in two and a half?" They'll almost always choose the time with a half in it, so make that one the time you want. With this choice, you have their buy-in and that goes a long way in cooperation.

Second, *your child is really involved in something at the moment.* When you want your child to do something, say it clearly *and give them time to process and respond.* Many parents say, "Come on, it's time to go. I said come here. Now. Let's go. Did you hear me? Come on!" All this in a twenty-second time frame. It takes the average toddler thirty seconds to hear, process, and respond. You need only say it once. (Of course, after thirty seconds, your kid could just be digging his heels in and ignoring you.) We usually don't like it when our toddlers demand we drop everything that second to attend to them. We ask them to hold on and practice patience. Practice what you preach. Give them the opportunity to finish up what they are doing. Most of the time, they'll come in short order. "I can see you're finishing up playing with your cars. As soon as you're done, let's go to the potty."

In this same category as the second point above is the child who is afraid to miss something while going to the bathroom. This is probably the number one cause of accidents in both the early stages and later. Children get very involved and either forget to think about whether they need the potty or don't want to miss out. There are a couple of ways to deal with this. You can have the activity come with you: "You can bring your truck with you to the bathroom." You can also directly address the activity (think in toddler-brain here): "Truck, you wait here. Pascal's going to pee and be right back." Addressing inanimate objects is a great tool for the first month of potty training: "Do you want to show your bear how you pee? Let's bring him to watch." Kids love this. You can set up their favorite dolls or stuffed animals in front of the potty to "teach" them how to do it. Be creative and think like a child. If you're watching a video, have the video "wait" by pausing it.

So, yes, your child may pee and poop through a couple of pairs of pants. This is to be expected. But if your child has peed (or pooped) in more than two pairs, it's time to go back to naked bum. While your child is still processing all the new information and we want to give them some time to figure things out, peeing and, especially, pooping in pants becomes a habit before you can say boo. In fact, I don't suggest even attempting pants until you get a good poop in the potty.

If you find yourself losing patience, take a breather. As they say, "If you're going through hell, for God's sake, keep going." This can be intense for you for a few days but it's infinitely better than extending potty training into a year or more.

Block 2 is not only about your child learning. You should be learning as well. Plan not only to learn your child's signals and pee-pee dance but also to learn their pee patterns. Some kids can drink 4 ounces of juice and pee seven times in the next hour. Other kids can drink four full cups and hold it for six hours. The whole goal here is to find a rhythm to your child's day and figure out where the potty fits in. If you have a frequent pee-er, you may not want to go anywhere for a while after that first glass of water. But if you know you have a camel, run a couple of errands. Of course, you're not going to know your child's pee habits perfectly after only a few days, but it's the eventual goal.

If there is some minor resistance during block 2, it's most likely the result of pure "toddlerness." There has been a change in routine. Remember that all your child has ever known is a diaper. Since they were a few hours old, they have worn one. They're a little attached, and it's okay. This is just something to keep in the back of your mind.

When facing resistance, most parents potty training on their own give up, often by deciding their child is not ready. Nothing could be further from the truth. If your child is capable of fighting for something they want, they're more than ready for potty training. Resistance can result in a short period of unpleasantness, but then it's done and you're over the hump.

> End result: Child can pee and poop with pants, shorts, or leggings on but commando (no underwear yet). This is with prompting or without prompting.

Block 3

This block of learning should be about solidifying the skills. It also brings small outings into the mix. Again, please don't confuse days with blocks. Block 3 might start on your second day of potty training. More likely, though, it's going to start somewhere around days 4 through 10. I'm only mentioning days because I know you need a marker, but try to let the day thing go. Block 3 brings more of the same: watching and prompting. By this time, you can have any combination of things happening. You could have a clear sense of your child getting it, or you could still be lingering somewhere else on the confidence time line. It's all good. A few days ago, your child had no concept of where pee and poop went. As I discussed in block 2, resistance could potentially kick up. Or you could be all set to take an eight-hour cross-country flight without diapers. The important thing is to stay calm no matter where you find yourself in the process.

There's no better way to help your child hone their potty skills than to take them outside the norm. In this case, that means leaving the house for short outings. For many of you, this is going to coincide with day care. Day care, like poop, can be one of the most frustrating aspects of potty training. So, also like poop, I gave it its own glorious chapter (chapter 12, "Day Care Struggles"). I think it's helpful to remember that potty training isn't a transferable skill at first. Just because they're good at home doesn't mean they won't get tripped up in different situations. As with walking, we don't expect a child to be able to handle themselves across many different terrains at first. Potty training can hit some snafus in new situations.

LEAVING HOME FOR THE NEWLY POTTY TRAINED

As you get ready for any sort of outing, be sure you get a good pee before leaving the house. I'm not suggesting bugging your child to pee. Rather, wait to leave until you get that pee and then hit the road. Again, firm directives work best: "You need to pee before we leave the house, because I will not like it if you pee in the car." If you're pretty sure you have an 11:00 a.m. pooper, don't leave around then. (Remember, this isn't forever; you are still starting out.)

Bring an extra outfit and wipes. Hell, bring the potty chair! I'm a huge advocate of bringing the potty chair or insert in the car. It doesn't weigh much, and even if your kid poops, you just bring it home. It's not much different from carrying around a poopy diaper. Plan for accidents. They're going to happen, and it's okay. But chances are that if you keep your small outings small, you may not have any.

An awesome couple I once worked with took on potty training like a Navy SEAL assignment. They had a total tag team plan. The dad took the child out on trial runs all day on the second and third days. They went to Target and the market and the library, all just for restroom practice. And it went really well. I just loved their dedication to getting this down, no matter what the environment. Something to consider.

Blocks 2 and 3 are by far your hardest chunks of learning. You, the parent, may be feeling insane or incredibly intense. It's normal, but try to chill out. I cannot say this enough: this process can look like a full-blown disaster and then clear up. I cannot tell you the amount of mail I get in which a mom goes from being nearly in tears to, "Wow. Never mind, he just sat and peed."

Somewhere during potty training, things are going to seem off.

I'm convinced this is where most parents who try to wing it totally f**k it up. Pay close attention. The entire crux of potty training is in the next two sections. They address the areas where parents most commonly go wrong: rushing, not prompting, and overprompting.

Do not overprompt or hover. Almost all resistance is because there is too much "process" in the process. Certainly some children are really difficult to potty train. However, in 95 percent of the people I've worked with, resistance is the result of hovering parents. Instead of blindly prompting, remember that you are not ASKING if they have to go; instead look for signals. Try to find a pattern and a rhythm. If you need to, keep a mental note to not prompt more than once per half-hour. Never, ever should the prompting take on a begging, cajoling, or negotiating tone. You are not playing *Let's Make a Deal*; you are prompting your child to sit and pee. Period. This can be done firmly without being done meanly. If you find yourself begging, cajoling, or negotiating, back off immediately. Once you start negotiating, your child will think they have a choice in this whole potty training thing, and things will go downhill very quickly.

PROMPTING

A common complaint I hear a few days into potty training is something along the lines of, "He's doing fine but only when we tell him to go. Is this kid EVER going to tell us when he has to go?"

My answer is: "OF COURSE he will!"

But right now, in the early stages of potty training, your child needs you. It still counts if they pee in the potty because you tell them to. Like any other learning they have done or will do, they need you—the parent—as a crutch. Remember that when your child learned to walk, they had to hold your hands at first for both the physical support and the comfort. Then they took a few tentative steps away from you but quickly needed your hand again. In strange environments, they hold your hand to tug you along to where they want to investigate. *Prompting is holding their hand.*

Some kids might immediately start to self-initiate, but most build it slowly; usually about three weeks into the process, you can start counting on self-initiating. Until then, it will be a few days of you always prompting. Then there will be a few days during which they tell you maybe one or two times that they have to go. Then, every once in a while, they will sit on their own and do their business. It will continue to build. And in strange situations, you may have to do some more hand holding. And one day you will wake up and not have potty training on the brain. I swear to God, this day will come.

When to Prompt

The big trick with prompting is to not overprompt. Ninety percent of all resistance is caused by overprompting. So the question becomes how often to prompt without slipping into overprompting (aka bugging, nagging, and generally overtalking it).

While your child is learning to use the potty, you should be learning some things too: namely, your child's pee pattern. Some kids can drink 4 ounces of fluid and pee nine times in an hour. Other kids are camels and can drink 32 ounces of fluid and pee twice all day. Some children are camels until they "break the seal" (college drinking days, anyone?). Then it's nine times in an hour. Every kid is different. This pee pattern is going to let you get back to regularly scheduled life after potty training. If you know you have a big drinker and pee-er in the morning, don't go running errands first thing. If you know you have a camel, run like the wind to get your shopping done.

You will also be learning your child's particular pee-pee dance. Some kids have the classic hopping around, ants-in-the-pants dance. Other kids are crotch grabbers. Some kids get slow and silent. The first few days of potty training should get you acclimated to your child's particular dance. This is naturally a good time to prompt while simultaneously bringing the child's awareness to the dance. Say something like, "I can see you have to pee. You are holding your penis. Come, sit on the potty."

Remember: you are not asking your child if they have to pee. You are prompting them to use the potty.

There are some other very natural, and therefore low-pressure, times to prompt. These are times we all go pee, so the prompts don't have a nagging quality to them and tend not to interrupt the child in the middle of something. These are called "easy catches," and they occur upon awakening and before sleep, before leaving (anywhere) and upon arrival (anywhere), before and after prolonged sitting (high chair, car seat, laps, couches), and before and after an engaging activity (especially ANY screen time).

It's also okay and very natural to hold off on an activity until your child pees, especially when you are certain they will need to. You might say something like, "Sure, we can leave for our walk as soon as you pee," or, "Yes, you can watch Elmo. Sit and pee first and let me know when you're done." This is not to be confused with bribery or rewarding, which would look something like, "I'll let you watch Elmo if you sit and pee for Mommy." Don't slip into bribery. You will end up with a power struggle.

It's also helpful to prompt as part of a cluster of other things. "Please pick up your blocks. It's time for lunch. Go sit on the potty, and then we'll wash hands." This does two things: it puts potty training in the normal realm of "things you just do," and it keeps your tone and vibe normal. I know this is shocking, but parents can get shrill and anxious around potty training. A brilliant mom I once worked with found that talking about using the potty as something "helpful" worked wonders. Her daughter loves being helpful so she would phrase it as, "Put your fork on the table. Put your cup on the table. Go sit and pee. Thank you. You are such a big help."

The delicate dance of prompting without overprompting is an important one. It's also important to remember that this is temporary. Many parents try to rush the self-initiation and end up with a lot of accidents. You don't want to do this. If your child doesn't have a lot of success to build on, their little mind will go to some version of "I suck at this. I'm not even going to try anymore." (I call it the inner "f**k it.") You are building a tower of success. If you start kicking out blocks from the foundation, the tower will tumble.

Overprompting and Backing Off

Overprompting usually goes down like this: around the fourth or fifth day into potty training, "I don't know what happened! It was totally clicking. She HAD it. She was sitting and peeing and pooping. Now, all of a sudden, she won't sit on the potty when I prompt her and she's having accidents all over the place. HELP!"

When you are potty training, there comes a time when you have to hand control over to your child. Usually this is within the first week. A really good sign that your child wants you out of their business is when they "had it" and all of a sudden resists or starts to have tons of accidents.

The learning phase of anything sucks. No one wants to "be learning"; we like to "have learned."

This is a catch-22, and it's scary as hell. You need to give control over to them, and they've not yet proven they can handle it. Failing to turn over control at the right time is a classic mistake in potty training. Because your child isn't self-initiating and going on their own, you figure you have to keep at them.

In reality, what we need to do is give them room to make the right choice for themselves. If you are constantly at them—watching, hovering, trying to help—they have no room to make this their own. This doesn't mean you leave it totally up to them. Prompting is going to be necessary for a bit longer. You must prompt without overprompting, which sounds awfully Yoda-ish, but it's true.

Here's the trick: I call it the *throw-away prompt*: toss the prompts out there with as little energy as possible—something like, "I can see you have to pee. There's your potty." Then drop the matter. Walk away and let it go mentally and physically. Now they can make their own choice, which means there's nothing to resist. If you don't care, there's nothing for them to fight. Of course you do care, but you have to give your child the room to learn how to use the potty, choose to do so, and do it themselves. The lofty reason for this is that it makes the accomplishment their own. The reality is that it's easier this way. Sometimes, you have to take the process out of the process.

Here's a direct quote from a former client, Alisha:

I definitely think the hands-off approach is what we needed here. I think experimenting a bit really helped us to figure a few things out. First, we needed to take the potty training out of potty training, if that makes sense at all. I think once we hit a snag Friday, we all got too focused on it, and everyone was hyperaware of every poop/pee/toot that came out of her and we weren't just being a family and spending time together. Tried the complete opposite today. Didn't really talk much about it at all except when I needed to, and kept it short and sweet. I guess the message she is sending me is that she can do it without me and actually does better that way. If I act at all available to help her, she then uses me like a crutch and suddenly can't do anything by herself anymore.

Exactly!

WHAT YOU ARE LOOKING FOR:
At the end of block 3 you should have some confidence in being able to leave the house with your child with clothes on. You can plan slightly longer outings, maybe to a friend's house. Be mindful, though, that you still watch your child for signals. It should already be getting easier to see those signals, but don't get engrossed in a conversation in another room. And bring the potty in the car. I remember bringing it to the beach with Pascal. He actually got out of the water to use his potty! I was impressed that he didn't just pee in the water! I don't think it's necessary to bring the potty into buildings that do have toilets. You don't want to foster any weird attachment to just that one potty (toddlers are notorious for weirdness). I would advise you to keep the potty in the back of the

car when you're out. You can pee in parking lots, behind trees, or whenever you are out and about. I'll address public restrooms later. This is temporary. Your time frame for getting to the potty will keep increasing, and soon your child will be able to hold their pee and poop until you can get to a regular toilet.

Early in potty training, the pre-pee warning progression will cap off at around five to ten seconds (meaning that at least for now, when your child signals that they have to pee, you have five to ten seconds to get them to the potty). I have found that they can wait a little longer if you at least respond. Say you're doing dishes in the kitchen and they're in the playroom. If they call out that they need to pee, you would say as you're running to them, "I'm coming. Please hold it." You will still need to keep an eye on your child at least for another month (although not with the intensity of the first day). Most likely, your child will signal with a pee-pee dance, but if not, you've gotten the pee pattern down and know to prompt at certain times.

Usually a few weeks of commando and bringing along the potty is sufficient. After a month, you should be fine. Of course, gauge it for yourself. If you think you need it longer, go for it. Once again, think of how you can support your child in success. You want to line up everything in your and your child's favor!

> End result: Going various different places, with clothes on, still with no undies, with prompting or without. You can bring the little potty with you in the car to support them in this process.

Blocks 4, 5, and 6 . . . to Infinity and Beyond!

By now, you should be seeing quantifiable progress. It will continue to get easier and easier. Rather than keeping notes (for the love of God, please don't keep a pee log!) strive for a rhythm. You want to be in harmony with your child, not on them and bugging them all day long. The parents who do best tend to be laid-back and rely on their intuition. There's really no rule book here, just learning.

You will keep building on success. I often refer to this as "stacking successes." You want to pay close attention to your child's successes and not harp on the failures. If your child is making it to the potty more often than not, it's good. If they have five pees on the pot and two misses, that's good. Yes, it needs improvement, but it's good. It's human nature to pick out the bad. I used to own a children's clothing store. Almost all of my customers were awesome, but still, I would go home bitching about the one customer who blew my day. We all do this, but try to step out of it while potty training. Yes, we want to fix problems, but we don't want to come down on the child all the time.

These may very well be the weirdest, hardest few days of your parenting career. It can be tedious, doing this dance of balancing vigilance with casualness. It will feel like it's taking a lot longer than it is. In the grand scheme, you're potty training in a short period of time. I cringe when I see people taking a year to potty train. They will encounter the same struggles you will, only theirs will be super-prolonged.

Should things seem to be progressing but at a slower rate than you anticipated, that's okay. Continue at a slower rate. If there appears to be a major snafu and you're seeing *no* progress, the rest of this book is troubleshooting and different pottying scenarios. Potty training isn't rocket science, but it isn't a single simple scenario either. Every child is different, and I think I've seen every possible situation. I will say that almost all problems can be solved by relieving any kind of pressure, whether pressure to maintain a social calendar, to prove yourself, to do this right, or to potty train in exactly three days or fewer.

Most people don't have any trouble at all. Most likely, your child's signals will be pretty clear to both of you. You will probably feel a new bond with this Big Kid. You are going to be amazed at your kid's self-pride. You are going to be blown away by what they are capable of. This is going to rock your world! One of the absolute coolest things I've found about potty training is it gives you a look into your child's psyche. You gain insight into your child's learning methods and curve, and that's wonderful!

Not every child learns the same way. Good teachers know this. When a student isn't learning, they find a back door to teaching and get creative. So many parents give potty training a whirl—a half-assed whirl, usually—and are quick to throw a diaper back on because their child, they say, "isn't getting it." When your child isn't learning something, you get creative with the teaching. You don't ditch it.

We have no way to know how your child will learn this until you jump in. It's important to remember that this is probably the first thing you are actively teaching and the first thing they are actively learning. That is to say, this is the first case in which you're teaching and they're learning something that must take place in a certain order and for which there really is only one right outcome. The more you can look at potty training as just something you are teaching your child, the better off you are going to be.

Underpants, self-initiation, and night and nap dryness all blend into the recipe at around three weeks after your starting date. (Night training has its own chapter, so I won't go into much here.) We've talked a little about self-initiation, another area that trips parents up. I'll discuss this further in chapter 9, "Block 4 and All the Rest," but for now, just remember that even if your child IS indicating to you that they have to pee or poop, they usually aren't very reliable at this stage, so don't totally back off from prompting.

Let's look at undies here and the best way to start wearing them. It's best to start with JUST undies at home. As I've mentioned, sometimes you have to rush this process because of day care or preschool. Just do your best. I've found that character undies work really well if you're so inclined. Most kids have some integrity about not peeing on their favorite characters, so use that to your advantage.

There are a couple of different scenarios here. One is that your child is home with you for a bit of time, maybe a week, but has to go back to day care at some point. In this case, assuming all is going well, you can start to try undies a few days in. If your child wets them right away, I'd take them off. It can feel sketchy with a time crunch but the stronger the foundation of peeing without them, the better off they'll be when they have to.

Another scenario is that you only have a few days to potty train. Since this is the hardest scenario, I encourage taking as many days as possible to learn this at home. It's a lot to throw at a child to learn a big new skill, undo a lifelong habit of diapers, and deal with undies and clothing in a day care setting. But if you're stuck, you have to introduce undies sooner than I'd prefer. Again, try JUST the undies at home first and keep a keen eye on your child so you can assist when you see the signs.

And the third scenario is when your child doesn't go to day care and is home all day with you or a caregiver. In this scenario, you don't have to rush undies at all. I wouldn't stress if even a lot of time goes by and your child doesn't want or do well with undies. Adding undies to the mix can be tricky, so use your parental intuition and judgment. Push the limits a little. Don't be fearful. Remember, above all, that your vibe and energy are running the show.

To recap, progressing through the blocks of learning is what's important. Don't track this by days. Make sure to meet the goals of each block before moving on. The transition points from pre-potty training to block 1, and from block 1 to block 2 are where most parents panic. It's okay. Move through those transitions. You are looking for forward movement, not perfection. If your child races to the potty but has an accident on the way, that's awesome; they were moving in the right direction. Evaluate success through the lens of a teacher who is looking for progress.

Roughly speaking, blocks 1, 2, and 3 typically take three to seven days, maybe slightly longer. If you feel like you're getting stuck in a block, please check out all of my resources. I have tons of reels on my IG feed, videos on YouTube, and the *Oh Crap! Potty Training* podcast.

CHAPTER 6

Nighttime Training

Okay! Night and naptime potty training. (This chapter refers to nap as well as night. For brevity, I say just *nighttime*.) Before we launch into nighttime training, note that I have separated out nighttime from daytime because to potty train for both at once looks overwhelming to most parents, particularly those who are single or work full time out of the home. *But potty training for night and day at the same time is the most effective way to potty train.* It will be more chaotic for a few days, but in the long run, you will have almost zero hassles down the road. When there is no backup—no other option—there are no power struggles, and there's less confusion and less withholding of pee and poop. When you make using the potty the new way of doing things day AND night, it becomes second nature much faster. It's totally up to you, and I won't lie: it's a more difficult first week, but I throw it out there that tackling day and night at the same time is better in the long run. I would not do night and day together if both parents work outside the home and you have a limited time window to be at home with your child. If you do choose to do both night and day together, clearly the blocks of learning would be out of order as you're taking on block 6 at the same time as block 1. Let's jump in and take this slow because this can get confusing for a lot of parents.

Is Night Training Necessary?

Yes. Or maybe no. If you are potty training your toddler under the age of three, you have some wiggle room. Many, many children start staying dry on their own as they get better and better at holding and consolidating during the day. I like to leave room for this to happen because it's true for many kids and obviously way easier on you. However, if your child gets to three and is showing no indication of starting to stay dry on their own, you must attend to night training. If it hasn't naturally occurred by then, *you must attend to it*. The bladder is being developed at this age, and if it develops fully without the practice of holding and consolidating, those muscles will atrophy, and you may struggle with longer-term bed-wetting.

I can in no way know for certain what is true for every single child. But I can see trends in the thousands of kids I have worked with. A very real and serious trend I see is that once a child is past the age of four, night training becomes incredibly difficult.

This is a sticky point for a lot of parents. Pediatricians will often tell you not to worry about it, that it will happen on its own. There is also a new cultural idea making the rounds on social media that it's very normal to regularly wet the bed until the age of ten. This is not normal. Having to use a pull-up at the age of six or seven or even ten isn't normal. Yes, bed-wetting has existed forever and we'll get to that in a minute. But this is not the norm. I think it's worth mentioning that I work with a lot of pediatricians whose own kids are seven or older and still in diapers at night. It's always best to ditch all diapers as soon as you have the capacity to do so. But night training can be wonky because there *really* is an issue of whether the child's bladder is able to hold and consolidate for such a long time. As much as I hate the "wait till they're ready" sound bite, this does come into question when we're talking about holding pee for ten or more hours. A really good indicator that a child is ready for night training is when they start staying dry for their nap. *However, this isn't true for every kid.* So don't wait for that necessarily, but should your child start staying dry during naps, go for it!

There is no such thing as *just* nap training. You can always try to go without a diaper for a nap, but there is *nothing* we can do to assist the child (i.e., you can't wake a child midnap to help them empty their bladder).

Putting aside the potty training needs of neurodivergent kids (see chapter 16 for more on this subject) as well as some truly tough and rare neurotypical cases, the sheer volume of kids currently over four years old in night diapers is not right. It's not an issue of the kids not being able to do it. It's an issue of the wicking of disposables, the child not feeling the wetness, and the aggressive marketing on the part of the big diaper companies.

So, no. You don't have to dive into night training if you don't feel up to it yourself. Or if your child has been struggling with sleep. Or if you're struggling with sleep. But I can't say it enough: *Do not go past three and a half years old without attending to it.*

A random side note here is that if you are over thirty-two weeks pregnant, it's totally cool to put off night training until the baby is around four to six weeks old. You need to rest, save energy for labor and birth, and adjust to life with a newborn. You can attend to night training when you are waking for night feedings for the baby. There is no reason to stress yourself out with night training right now. Unless, of course, you want to.

The next big question is, What is the goal of night training? We'll get to the how-to in a minute, but night training does involve waking the child for a sleepy dream pee. At first, the point of this is to literally help your child to catch the pee. This is brand-new to them, and nighttime is a long time to go without peeing. They will need to pee, and so in the beginning, it's up to us to catch it. Toddlers should be sleeping anywhere from nine to thirteen hours each night, a long time to go without peeing! Think about it; most adults wake up to pee at least once a night, and we are *skilled* at using the potty. But there's also a subconscious learning that happens: you wake when you have to pee. Many parents fear that the wakings will teach the child to depend on them in order to do this. I know this sounds logical but that's not what happens. They really do start to pick it up on their own.

The actual goal of night training is not actually sleeping through the night without peeing. Some kids, as with adults, may be able to. But for the majority, being able to get up when you have to pee is a better thing to think about. Through the years working with all different personalities, lifestyles, and differences, **I've found the best goal is this: the last adult standing pees the child before going to bed.** This is a really solid goal because it's doable over the long term should your child need a helping hand. The thing that is NOT sustainable is waking in the middle of the night.

I've searched and searched for the Magic Nighttime Trick, but it doesn't exist. There's no way around it. To train for nighttime, you have to carefully monitor fluid intake before bedtime and/or wake your child to pee. I wish there were a magic trick I could give you. I do, however, have some tips to make night training a lot easier on you. Before we get to that, here are a few things you'll need or need to do before you begin.

- Get some piddle pads, otherwise known as chux pads. These are great to duct-tape to the mattress in layers. Night training is going to involve some accidents for most kids, and this way you can just peel a layer off and not change sheets in the middle of the night.

- If your child is accustomed to a bottle or sippy cup or even an open cup full of milk or water right before bed, you'll want to break this habit. Having any liquid before bed will almost guarantee pee in the bed.

- Consider moving your child from the crib to a bed. I have many podcasts on the best way to do this. While it is possible for a child in a crib to be night trained, I think it's best to set your child up to be independent. Many times, by the time they call for you and you get there, they will have wet themselves.

- Use a nightlight. Perhaps you have blackout curtains or just a really dark room. A motion-sensitive nightlight or even a red light nightlight is useful for both you and the child to be able to see where they're going.

- Time to ditch the sleep sack. Sleep sacks make night training hard. If your child is using one and loves it, many parents turn the sleep sack into a pillow and it becomes a nighttime lovey.

- Use two-piece PJs. For the time being, I highly suggest two-piece pajamas. One-piece PJs mean that much more futzing with clothing, potentially leading to a more awake child.

The Actual Work of Night Training

We begin with two wakings. I recommend 10:00 p.m. and 2:00 a.m. at first, though you can adjust as needed. This is assuming a rough 7:00 p.m. bedtime to a rough 6:00 a.m. wake time. You just want to be a few hours into sleep and a few hours away from waking time. Otherwise the child may wake fully, and no one wants a wide-awake toddler in the middle of the night. Unfortunately, the idea of waking to pee isn't something you can explain to the child in words. It has to be learned physically, through waking.

These should be sleepy pees. The potty chair should be next to the bed for the least disruption. The point of these wakings is to figure out when your child pees the most. Typically the major pee will be one or the other—either before or after midnight.

Monitor fluids about two to three hours before bedtime, making sure there's minimal intake (about one hour before nap). This can be hard on your child if you do it suddenly. If your kid is used to lots of fluid before bed, start by scaling back gradually before you attempt your first diaperless night.

The next part is simple but not necessarily easy. Once you ascertain when your child is peeing the most, try to get rid of that second wake-up. If they pee most at the earlier wake-up, that's awesome. You can start moving the time up until the last adult in the house goes to bed; that person can take the child to pee and most likely be all set for the night. If your child is peeing the most at the 2:00 a.m., you'll probably want to start moving the time closer to waking. When I say "start moving the time," move slowly, as in ten-minute increments every couple of nights. Again, a really good goal that is sustainable is having the last adult awake pee the child before bed. That's it in a nutshell.

Best Practices for the Actual Wakings

Let me give you some tips to help make this all go more smoothly and then we'll talk about some troubleshooting because we're talking about toddlers and smooth roads are hard to come by. The easiest, least disruptive way to go about handling these wakings is to set your cell phone alarm so you don't have the blaring alarm clock going off in the middle of the night. Have the potty chair next to the child's bed. It's best for the child to be bare-bummed for the first week or so, so I suggest at least no undies while night training. No undies or no pajama bottoms are the best subconscious reminder to not release pee. And they wouldn't do too much to contain a pee anyway.

Your child should still be in a sleepy state (this is not a conscious teaching moment). The harder part is holding up their limp weight. Mostly-asleep kids are like wet spaghetti—heavy, wet spaghetti. Get them to the potty, and then you can just hold them up and whisper for them to pee. I've always found it helpful to make a sshhhing noise (similar to the sound of peeing) in the child's ear. Even half-asleep, your child may indicate they don't have to pee; just put them back down.

Don't turn on bright lights and try to lug your child to the bathroom. If you do, you'll have yourself a wide-awake toddler party at 2:00 a.m. This shouldn't take more than five minutes. Many kids will say no or shake their head that they don't have to pee. That's okay, but here's the tricky part. They're very new at this so just because they say they don't have to pee now doesn't mean they won't have to in ten minutes. A good trick at this point is to tuck them back in and whisper in their ear, "Hold your pee till I come for you." I don't know why but this can be magical. I think whispering it goes right into their subconscious. It works for many kids.

Tips before Going to Bed

THE DOUBLE PEE

Getting two attempts at peeing before bed helps. Often in the nighttime routine, kids rush through peeing. Getting two pees around bedtime can truly empty the bladder. To do this, just pepper an extra pee into the nighttime routine. That might look like, "Okay, time to get ready for bed. Let's go pee and put PJs on and read. Then we'll brush teeth, last pee, wash hands, and I'll tuck you in." It also helps to ask to *hear* more pee. This seems to distract them from resistance to going into cooperation by listening to it.

ROLE-PLAY

This can be a lighthearted way to practice as part of your nighttime routine. You can have your child pretend to be asleep (goofy snoring noises included). Then you say, "Okay! You have the feeling to go pee! What do you do?" And they can practice getting up to use the potty. This can get silly, and that's okay.

MONITORING FLUIDS

You should avoid sippy cups and bottles at night (and actually during the day as well). The sucking action leads kids to take in more than they would if they were using a cup. A great trick I've learned for monitoring fluids is to buy tiny cups: sake cups, mini-teacups, or even shot glasses. This gives the illusion of a full glass, even though there's very little liquid in it. Also, kids love little things that are their size. I know quite a few moms who've developed a lovely nighttime tea ritual with their kids. (Chamomile tea is widely accepted as promoting sleep and calm.) Little cups also come in handy for the classic bedtime stall, "I need a drink of water." If your kid does this, you can use a tiny cup to give them a drink without worrying they're taking in too much fluid.

Planning for a reduction in fluids before bed has been one of the most controversial points of my book. I often have parents screaming in all caps on the Internet that I am suggesting YOU DEHYDRATE YOUR CHILD. I want to be very clear. I am not suggesting you dehydrate your child. But what we can do is focus on making sure they have fluids at appropriate times so they won't be slugging down fluids right before bed or nap.

I like to think of the day in terms of two upside-down pyramids, one spanning the time from waking to nap and the other, from nap waking to sleep. The width of the bottom of the pyramid represents the amount of fluid your child should be drinking so you want to flip that; go heavy on fluids upon awakening and then taper to almost nothing about an hour before nap and at least two hours before bedtime. If your child is used to having a big glass of something with dinner, this habit needs to change. Making the change can be tricky for a day or so, but your child will get used to it. You'll then need to watch fluids from dinner on. Monitoring fluids before sleep will naturally make your child thirstier in the morning, which works perfectly with the fluid pyramid. Most kids have drinking patterns that resemble right-side-up pyramids. What happens is that they are very busy little beings, and as they start to settle down for nap or bedtime, they suddenly realize they're thirsty. So making time for drinking well before nap and bedtime will help immensely with not peeing during sleep. I find it helpful to get into this routine well before beginning nighttime training.

If you are still nursing intermittently throughout the night, night training could be a little trickier. Generally, however, most kids at this age are nursing for comfort rather than volume, so they may not be taking in much fluid. Also, you could have your child pee before or after nursing. Pick whichever option better fits your child. Some kids like to pee before nursing; most prefer it afterward. Either is fine, but the trick is consistency.

SLEEPING

If you are co-sleeping, the good news is that night training is much easier. Your child has no travel time and usually gets restless right before needing to pee, which will help alert you to the situation. It's also a lot easier on you if all you need to do is roll over as opposed to walking down the hall to your child's room. That said, though, if you haven't ever had the desire to co-sleep, I wouldn't recommend starting just to make night training easier.

If your child is a very light sleeper and wakes fully at the drop of a pin, you have two choices: you can be vigilant about monitoring fluids or delay night training. I'm not a huge fan of delayed night training, but sleep trumps potty training. If your child is a super-heavy sleeper, you might want to look into potty alarms. There are many to choose from, but typically these kids need an assist because they can sleep right through the feeling of having to go pee.

Many parents are concerned because they've put in a *lot* of work to have good sleepers, so the idea of purposely waking a child feels all kinds of wonky to them. I applaud any parent who has gotten sleep down pat. But these are not meant to be wide-awake pees, and because you've put in the work to have a good sleeper, I can almost guarantee that they'll have no problem with the dream pee wakings.

Toddlers should be in bed around 7:00 p.m. This can be difficult with schedules and both parents working outside the home, but you should move heaven and earth to make this happen. Too little sleep wreaks havoc on their mood, skill building, and developing brain.

THE "HORMONE THING"

Perhaps you've heard about "the hormone thing," or your pediatrician has said, "Don't worry about night training. There's the hormone thing." About ten years ago, that's all I was hearing and those exact words: "the hormone thing." No one could tell me what the hormone thing was or what it had to do with night training. I thought it was odd that everyone was talking about it and yet no one seemed to know what it was. So I did a little digging.

The hormone thing is ADH, the antidiuretic hormone that is released at night. This hormone slows down urine production so we can, for the most part, sleep through the night. I sleep eight hours a night and get up to pee once. However, an eight-hour span during the day will yield about 80 million pees. Okay, not 80 million but a lot more than one. Kids don't have this as a baby and grow into it. A small portion of the population never grows into it, and that's why they are bed-wetters. We can never know for certain exactly when kids grow into this but it's somewhere between fifteen months and typically three years. What we do know is two things that really affect the release of this hormone: circadian rhythm and attention deficit hyperactivity disorder (ADHD).

Circadian rhythm is your twenty-four-hour body clock. It's a big topic, but suffice it to say that we all have a perfect range in which sleep is ideal. You can tell you've hit this range if you fall asleep within five to ten minutes of going to bed. And you tend to sleep more soundly. For example, I've learned that I *must* be in bed by 10:00 p.m. I have a tight range for this: I have until 10:15 p.m. to go to sleep. If I stay up later than that, I'm on another cycle and it's hard for me to get to sleep until around 2:00 a.m. It's not impossible, but I'll toss and turn a lot more.

Our kids are the same way. If your child goes to bed but stays awake and talking to themselves for an hour, they are on the wrong cycle. After working with many, many sleep experts, I can assure you the answer is almost always earlier sleep, not later sleep. Toddlers should be in bed by 7:00 p.m. and the latest at 7:30 p.m. in order to get the best rest. In many cases, it may be earlier. I know this can be tricky depending on your work and life, but it's worth strategizing ways to make that happen. (I expand on this concept a lot on my podcast.) If your child is not on the right circadian sleep cycle for them, that ADH hormone won't be released. It's released with melatonin, which is also contingent on the right sleep cycle. The moral of the story is that if you're struggling with night training, start moving your child's bedtime earlier in ten-minute increments to see if you can hit the sweet spot. I've worked with many families who doubt this; they swear their child is not tired and needs a later bedtime, and they are struggling with night training. We start moving that bedtime earlier, and suddenly the child falls asleep quickly and night training resolves. If your child is peeing many times during the night, that means ADH is not being released. In this case, try an earlier bedtime, or you may have to hold off night training until it is. This is a hard concept to wrap your head around; an earlier bedtime is your best bet, but it's not a guarantee.

People with ADHD tend to have flipped circadian rhythms: they tend to be the night owls, which means that the ADH won't be released. Many kids with ADHD do struggle with night training. What's really hard is that most kids won't get an official diagnosis until they're about four or five. If you suspect your child has ADHD, it's worth putting a good amount of work into sleeping at appropriate hours. It's doable, for sure, but it might take being really strict about your nighttime routine for a while.

How Long Should Night Training Take?

Night training can take anywhere from one to eight weeks. What we're looking for is patterns. Can your child hold their pee until you come? I can't describe it as anything else, but you should feel that you're making progress. If it feels all over the map, you've really tried, and you just can't get a handle on any pattern, it's okay to rediaper at night and hold off for a bit. Assuming you're continuing with night training, don't worry, eventually your child will either be able to hold it all night or will wake up to ask to pee. You'll know they're ready to go all night when they routinely say no or shake their head during the wake-up pee. Even if it starts to look as if they're able to hold it all night, continue to monitor fluids in the evening. If they show the ability to wake up by themselves to pee, you don't have to be so vigilant. Either scenario is equally acceptable.

Nighttime potty training can take longer than daytime potty training, but that is not always so. Each child is different, and each parent's level of commitment is different. Be gentle with yourself and realistic with your capabilities. As with day training, repetition and consistency are the most important factors.

If you absolutely know you are unable to wake up to assist your child, then you may need to be an ultravigilant fluid monitor before bed. The reverse is also true: if you simply cannot monitor fluids before bed, commit to waking up. You do need to deal with night training at some point. Many parents think it will just happen and then get stuck later on.

I get two questions about this regularly. The first is, "I need my sleep. There's no way in hell I'm waking up. What else can I do?" My answer is that you probably need to be very vigilant about monitoring fluids well before bedtime. The second question is sort of the flip side of the first one: "My child absolutely needs their bottle/sippy cup of water/milk/juice before bed. What else can I do?" In this case, be prepared for night training to not go well. That much fluid right before bed will result in many pees, and it will be hard to get a handle on any sort of pattern.

Here are a few closing points about night training:

- Earlier wake-ups: A disturbing thing for many parents is a child who wakes at 5:00 a.m. to pee. But see? The trouble with teaching your kid to feel the sensation of peeing is that now they feel the sensation of peeing. We all have a 4:00 or 5:00 a.m. pee in us. The difference is as adults, we can either hold it or pee and go back to sleep. Our little ones can't. Most kids start waking up earlier because they have to pee. This will level off after a few weeks, and you'll be back to their normal wake-up.
- Teething: If your child is teething, night training goes to hell in a handbasket. Try to coast through the teething period but if you need to rediaper, it's okay.
- Time changes (e.g., travel, daylight savings, and any major disruption in routine): Also hell in a handbasket. My advice is to coast through these as best you can.

BUT IF IT ALL GOES SIDEWAYS, let's say you've done everything. You are monitoring fluids, you're doing the two wake-ups, you're trying really effing hard, and no matter what, you can't find a pattern, there's pee and laundry and ohmigod please stop. Shhh. Take a breath. I think night training is important. But I also think your mental health is important and sleep is key.

Don't think, "If I only got up four and a half minutes sooner, I could have caught it." I call that "chasing time," the illusion that if we only did XYZ, then it'd be okay. Do the consistent 10:00 p.m. and 2:00 a.m. wake-ups. If there's anything out of that realm, let it go. Do not do more than two wake-ups. That's getting crazy, and it doesn't help anything. If you have given it a really solid go and you're still all over the map, REDIAPER. It's okay. With night training, there's not the mixed message of using a diaper. Some bladders are really not ready to hold through the night. Sometimes, that ADH isn't released. If it's all gone sideways and you're crying and can't deal: REDIAPER. In this scenario, I'd rather have everyone sleeping and not stressed.

The Last Few Nuggets of Night Training

Bear in mind that night training isn't an exact science. There will be nights when you're all out having fun, past bedtime, and your child is downing juice boxes like it's their job. Just know that on some nights, you might have to go back to a wake-up once in a while when life gets a little out of whack. I want to reassure you: night training takes some time and effort, for sure. But sleep always trumps potty training. I want you and your littles well rested above and beyond anything.

And a final note about a scenario that has become common: the child wakes with the feeling of having to pee and goes to the parents' room for help. The parents are annoyed that the kid doesn't just use the potty. Dude, this is a best-case scenario. They're little and need help. Remember, this is all temporary. All of it.

CHAPTER 7

Block 1 Drama

In this chapter, I address the common problems in the first week of potty training. If you are having difficulties, read through all the drama chapters. Problems can crop up at any point in potty training, not just during block 1. Separating problems by block is just my attempt to keep an overwhelming amount of information semiorganized. I typically see certain problems in certain blocks, but you may experience something different, so it's best to read through them all. And don't forget to turn to chapter 17, "Random Tips and Questions," for advice.

So you are making your way through block 1 of potty training, and I'm sure you are exhausted. You are most likely reading this chapter because you are unsure of how things are going. Or you know for a fact things are not going well. You may have a great feeling, or maybe not so great. Or confused. Or unsure. I'm sure you will run the gamut of emotions for the next week. Regardless of how you're feeling about potty training, do not let a successful (or failed) poop or pee in the potty determine your emotional state. In fact, it's a good idea never to let your toddler's behavior dictate your emotional state, though I know that's easier said than done. Remember, though, that potty training progress is not a measurement of your parenting abilities or of how smart your child is.

So let's see where you're at and what, if anything, you need to do differently. Remember the time line of potty training: Clueless, to I Peed, to I'm Peeing, to I Have to Go Pee. We are looking for progress, not perfection. I'm also going to refer alternately to "blocks" and "days," because no matter how much I want you to avoid tracking progress by days, you are going to.

Honestly, there are truly no disasters in the first couple of days of potty training because it's too new. You are changing a routine, a habit that has been in place for all of their lives, short as that may be. That's not going to happen in a day.

No Poop

The most common cause for a parental freak-out is not getting a poop on the first day. You may have noticed that poop has its very own chapter in this book because it's that big a freaking deal. Do not worry if there's no poop on the first day. Your child was most likely a once-, twice-, or three-times-a-day pooper when they were diapered. Almost every child I've ever worked with goes down to one poop a day during potty training. I think this consolidation of poops is natural. Most adults poop only once a day, if that. There's nothing to worry about from a medical standpoint if your kid has a day or two of no pooping. For many kids, that first day of potty training is very strange—all this focus on a previously unnoticed thing—and there's bound to be some performance anxiety.

If there's no poop, don't sweat it. Carry on like normal. Be aware, though, that a poop is most certainly coming at some point. Go look over chapter 10, "Poop," and see if anything there pops out at you. But honestly, especially on the first day, this is normal. It's important to note your nonverbal communication. If you are getting anxious about no poop, your child will most likely absorb that, and it won't help things.

Standing to Poop

Maybe you noticed this while your child was still in a diaper, or maybe it's something they're doing as you start potty training. Whatever the case may be, some kids are used to pooping standing up. If this seems to be your child, it's not a big deal. Don't try to force them to sit. Tell them it's totally okay for them to stand and that you'll help them catch the poop in the little insert cup that comes with the potty chair.

This is a bit awkward at first, but it's so worth it. This is how to bridge pooping standing up to sitting on the potty. It usually takes only a couple of days, and then they will begin to sit. It's far better to meet the child where they're at than butting heads trying to get them to sit. It will pass much more quickly with this little bridge trick, whereas I've seen the whole process implode trying to make them sit.

A Crazy Amount of Pee

If your child seemed to spend the whole day having accidents and not noticing, you are most likely overdoing the fluid consumption. Toddlers only need about a liter of fluid a day, and that includes water content from food. I highly recommend not using sippy cups at this point. A lot of kids suck for comfort, not just thirst. Sippy cups all over the place also make it harder to keep an eye on fluid intake. Make sure you're at a normal amount of liquid consumption. You should be monitoring fluid; this doesn't mean you should restrict liquids, it just means keeping an eye out for when and how much your child drinks relative to when and how much they pee so you can get a handle on their normal patterns.

Hardly Any Pee at All

Sometimes it's hard to make a kid drink. Try to notice if your child is really not drinking a lot or if they are just not peeing. If you only got a few pees on day 1, it's okay. Some children can really hold it. You don't have to assume they are purposely withholding the pee; maybe they can just really control their bladder. That's awesome. A child who can hold it is preferable to one who has to go every time there's even a small amount of pee in their bladder. Don't necessarily increase the fluid intake, but rather try to get a handle on their pee patterns. Start to get a sense of how long they can hold it after taking in fluid so you can predict the most appropriate times to prompt. My best friend's husband pees once a day, and he has never had a urinary tract infection. Some people are just camels. However, beware the camel: once the "seal" is broken, so to speak, many camels pee several times in a short period.

Absolutely No Awareness of Having Peed

Okay, you're chill with the notion of progress rather than perfection, you're relaxed that your kid isn't going to figure this all out in a day, you are not freaking out . . . but jeez Louise, this kid is showing *no* recognition that they just peed. WTH? This happens most often in children under twenty-two months. And I have never, ever seen a neurotypical kid, over the age of thirty months, be totally clueless. Regardless of your child's age, however, you'll want to make sure they truly are clueless rather than simply ignoring the pee. *Clueless* means . . . clueless. But the child who pees and pretends it didn't happen is *not* clueless. The truly clueless will pee while walking, slip on the puddle, fall, and have no idea what just happened. If, by the end of day 1, your child is still totally clueless, it's okay. All it means is that you are still in block 1.

Kid Pees and Pretends It Doesn't Happen

For this kid, remind them that pee goes in the potty. Frown or make an otherwise displeased facial expression and say, "No pee on the floor. Pee goes in the potty." Make those statements in that specific order, putting the *desired result* last. Kids tend to remember the last thing you said; it just seems to stick a little better. You don't want to be mean or reprimanding, but you do need to express that peeing on the floor is NOT good and peeing in the potty IS good.

Toddlers don't have a lot of emotional nuance at this age. They think in very black and white; big happy, big sad, and big mad is about all they know right now. So it's important to express yourself as to what is good and what is not so good. A neutral tone, meaning well, usually doesn't land. Again, I don't mean to be scolding or gruff. But be very clear that pee on the floor isn't great.

As for handling the accident, don't panic. You want to have your child help you clean up and sit on the potty to finish eliminating any pee they may have left in them. You can say something to the effect of, "I know you are learning, *and* your pee goes in the potty." *Do not* say, "It's okay." This phrase seems to imply permission (to pee on the floor) to some kids, even if what you really mean to express is, "My head is not going to explode or anything." Essentially, acknowledge that they're still learning while consistently reinforcing the idea that pee goes in the potty.

In the Two Seconds You Turned Your Back . . .

You've hardly been breathing, watching like a hawk for their pee-pee dance, a sign, a twitch, a signal. Nada. So *you* have to pee or get more coffee and the *two freaking seconds* your back is turned, they pee right there on the floor. Argh. How is this possible? Well, there's good news: this kid is well on their way to being potty trained. If they can hold it until the two seconds you turn your back, yep, that kid is almost done potty training. Think about it. Most likely, this is their way of asking for privacy. Remember, even though we don't think of it this way, a diaper conceals bodily functions, so it provides some privacy. Even though we see and clean up the messy diaper afterward, they still had privacy during the act of eliminating. Now their bum's in the breeze and there's no privacy. It's very cool to want privacy. It's the natural progression of potty training. So give them some. When you think it's about time for them to go, set them up on the potty and conveniently "forget" something in the other room. If they're using an insert on the big potty, it's the same deal, and you can close the bathroom door partially. Nine times out of ten, they'll pee the second you leave the room. This goes for poop too.

Also, whenever you have to pee during the beginning phases of potty training, bring your child with you. This is a great thing to do together. It normalizes and models the behavior. It's an all-around win.

The Kid Who Does Absolutely No Signaling Whatsoevah

Again, you're watching like a hawk, and for the life of you, you *cannot see* any sort of signal. I really do think almost all kids have a signal, even if it's just a pause in their action, but no worries if you can't spot one. I suggest putting more focus on learning their pee pattern.

Sir Dribbles-a-Lot

This kid is a dripping faucet. I mostly see dribblers in boys, for whatever reason. They can dribble a lot throughout the day, or it might occur right before they have to pee. This is not terribly worrisome in the first few days. You have to remember that yesterday, when and how to pee wasn't on their radar. Today they're getting used to a whole new ball game. We don't know for sure how your child peed when they were wearing a diaper. They might have let the pee out a little at a time until the diaper was full. For this kid, part of potty training is a natural consolidation of those little dribbly pees into one bigger one. It generally happens naturally as they get the hang of things.

The Kid Will Not Sit Long Enough to Pee

This is a common complaint. To counteract it, try doing something to engage them and keep their attention while they're on the potty. I offer suggestions like singing a song, counting to a particular number together (50 is a good one), or reading some books. A great phrase to use is, "I need to *hear* more pee." This resonates with kids better than "sit and finish your pee." I think it's because the kids are motivated to give you something other than the actual pee. They want to give you the *sound* of pee.

But this particular issue is also one of the places where parenting philosophies can kind of muck things up. Your child is getting to an age of limit testing, so you need to be firm and let your child know you mean business. For some parents, though, "being firm" feels sticky. Let me tell you that it's okay to be firm. You don't need to be mean to be firm. The less dancing around your child you do, the better. Sometimes parents go so over the top trying to get the child to sit and pee that it turns into serious entertainment for the kid. You don't want to set up that habit. Also, if you're bending over backward to get the kid to pee, it starts to smell like fear. Kids can smell fear a mile away, and it will either make *them* fearful or they will eat you for breakfast.

So what can you do? Some mild form of distraction is fine. I would stay away from screens, though. Don't use an iPad or phone or put the potty in front of a TV show and let your child just sit there. It may get them to sit, but it is way too passive. They are just getting the pee in the potty by chance because they happen to be sitting there. What they need to be learning is to act on the feeling of having to pee. A lot of parents do this out of desperation, but it just makes a bigger problem later, like your child asking to pee or saying they have to go poop every five minutes to get to use a device or watch a show. Remember that the idea is to normalize the use of the potty, not to make it into a big game or special thing.

The "Calm Jar"

This is a distraction that works well for a few different situations. Make a Calm Jar out of a mason jar or a clear plastic water bottle. Fill it with water, medium-sized glitter, and some oil or glycerin. The result is a sort of snow globe. Many parents use the Calm Jar in lieu of a time-out: the child can shake it and watch the glitter settle, which is calming and relaxing and takes a minute. I've found the Calm Jar to be excellent for kids who want to pop right up off the potty because it helps keep their interest, which keeps them seated. It's also great for the kid who's having trouble releasing pee or poop. This is the kid who sits on the potty but can't seem to let the pee go; then they pop up and pee on the floor. This kid is not screwing with you, even though it looks like it; they just need to sit longer and allow for the release. The Calm Jar will help them relax and let the pee start flowing.

Fear of the Potty

You've been casual and relaxed. You know you are not putting any pressure on your child. Still, your kid seems afraid of the potty. First, do *not* invalidate their feelings. Just like fear of the dark, the monster under the bed, or the vacuum, this is a real fear (however illogical it might be). We don't want to feed into it, but we don't want to invalidate it. Never ask your child if they are afraid of the potty. You will get a "yes," and there's nowhere to go from there. Here's the thing: if your child freaks out the minute you say the phrase *potty training* and show them the potty, what I have found is that it's not really the potty. Much like the word *time-out*, kids hear the phrase *potty training* all over the place. They are always listening even when it seems as if they're not. In my experience, that's what's behind the fear; having heard adults talking negatively about it all around them—not the actual potty chair, which is the most innocuous piece of plastic in your house. You can show them how it works with some water and they can dump it and that can help acclimate them to it.

Most kids aren't actually afraid of the potty. They are afraid of releasing, which we'll talk about in a minute. Also, you'll want to identify whether you're looking at a case of true fear or just a little bit of resistance. The child with a true, deep fear of the potty is rare and should be distinguished from a child who is showing resistance. In the case of a child with a true fear, the potty might as well be filled with boiling, molten lava; they want no part of it. The truly afraid child is the one who, right from the start, shrieked and hollered and had to be dragged to the potty. Note that a true fear shows up from the start of potty training. A child who starts resisting after using the potty a couple of times isn't truly *afraid*. Many children show resistance to the potty. Fear is something different. You will recognize it if you see it. I address the truly fearful child in chapter 16, "Special Circumstances, including Delays and Neurodiversity."

Fear of the Release

This can look like fear of the potty once they have the urge to pee. But it can also look as if they have to go: they are willing to sit and are willing participants, but then once they are sitting, they can't release. This isn't really fear per se; it's more like a glitch in the matrix. Some first-level fixes are using the potty in the bathroom and running the bath water, blowing bubbles, horse lips or raspberries, a small tickle or something you know makes your child laugh, blowing out a candle or a straw. All of these can relax the sphincter muscles as well as the mind/body and help them release their pee.

This is not the same as withholding pee. Withholding pee (and poop but we'll talk about that in the poop chapter) looks like the child has to pee but is not a willing participant. They will look frantic, have escalating behavior, and usually won't go anywhere near the potty. This is true anxiety and should be worked through. This is not a sign of "not ready," and rediapering won't help. I have more resources in the Don't Panic section.

So, are you sensing a theme here? In case you're too exhausted to put it together, I'll spell it out. *Nothing* is "wrong" the first day of potty training. Yesterday, your kid could pee and poop whenever and wherever the urge struck. Now you aren't letting them out of your sight, and they are expected to up and make this huge change. Just remember that.

There really is no such thing as a disaster in block 1. You should consider the first week of potty training as data collection. Even if they're doing really well, you still want to be learning those patterns and pee dances. This is how you can get back to "real life" and also share information with any other caregivers.

Also, never underestimate the power of sleep. Much will be accomplished in their sleep tonight. Information gets sorted out in the brain, and you can begin fresh in the morning. It's also totally fine to bounce back and forth between blocks 1 and 2 if you're seeing some success but feel like you need to solidify things a bit more.

CHAPTER 8

Block 2 and 3 Dilemmas

At this point, you should feel pretty comfortable that your child, while bare-bummed, can sit and pee on the potty. Remember that it's okay if you are still prompting. Prompting counts as success, and your child needs it. But don't overprompt (she says to the mom holding a knife). By now, you may have started with pants, or your child may still be butt-nekkid, or you may be doing a mix of the two.

Resistance!!! (Woo-hoo!)

This phase of potty training can bring about resistance. Regardless of what block you are on, resistance usually hits on the second day of potty training. Your kid is thinking, "This was okay when we started. But now . . . oh no, you might possibly be serious about this peeing-in-the-potty thing." The second day of potty training is most commonly when parents without a plan (ahem, they haven't read this book) give up. They think the resistance is a sign that the child is not ready. In reality, nothing could be further from the truth. If your child is able to put up a fight for something they want, they're more than ready to put pee in the potty.

I simply cannot tell you how many times I hear some version

of what former client Aislinn wrote: "I can't believe it! This looked like SUCH a disaster. I swear I was ready to give up. Thank god I didn't! Working through that resistance was not fun but now it's the fourth day and she's GOT IT! Yahoo!" The biggest reason for resistance is that you're "on it" too hard with your kid. You probably don't even realize how much pressure you're putting on your child, but most parents go through this at some point. You can't help it. You have potty on the brain, and you are on edge. Pressure is the number one killer of potty training, which is why I'm so adamant about allotting as much time to this learning as possible. If your kid is resisting, you are most likely overprompting.

Remember those two sections you read about prompting and backing off? The ones I said were really important? The ones you probably read way back two weeks ago when you were thinking about potty training in theory but weren't actually doing it yet? Read them again now that you're in the thick of it. Most problems can be solved with the information contained in those two sections. They'll help you strike the balance between overprompting and backing off.

For some children, everything clicks during the first few days of potty training, but for a good majority, it doesn't. I want to be CRYSTAL CLEAR HERE. In most cases, you simply need more time. I cannot tell you the number of people who book a private session with me on day 4 and then cancel it on day 6 because the child simply needed more time. This is a big transition and it's big learning.

Remember that all this was absolutely not on your child's radar a couple of days ago. I know I keep saying that, but it's important for you to take it to heart. We have to allow them time to learn this. Most parents realize this on some level, but still have a sort of lingering hope that everything will be signed, sealed, and delivered on the second or third day. As with any major milestone, mastering the potty takes time, and having a potty prodigy is highly unlikely. It can happen, yes. But I don't want you to feel weird or like you're doing a crappy job if it doesn't.

Side note for a second: I believe potty training pains are like labor pains: they get fuzzy around the edges with time. Most of the people who say their kid upped and decided not to wear diapers on their own have a kid older than yours. Or they're new in town. For whatever reason, you can't really verify their story. I hear about the "potty prodigy" all the time from moms on the playground. In reality, though, I hang around with a lot of moms and potty training is my job, and I've yet to see with my own eyes the kid who just potty trains themselves in hours. Just want you to know that so your head doesn't blow off.

Another important thing to remember is that every child has their own learning methods and curve. It's okay if they don't take to potty training as quickly as you expected. It doesn't mean your child is not smart or that you're not doing a great job.

Common Problems in Block 2

Having said that, there are some very common problems in block 2 of potty training.

PEEING RIGHT THROUGH THE PANTS

Your kid did *great* with block 1. *Great.* You knew that child was ready to move on. Got them up, took off the diaper, they peed first thing, you put 'em in some pants, and all they're doing is peeing right the hell through them all. It's 11:30 a.m., and you have seven pairs of soaking pants. WTF, Jamie?

Okay. Number one: Does your kid actually know how to manipulate their clothing? This is a big issue that we all tend to forget. I discussed it in chapter 4, but you probably glossed over it because it didn't seem very important when you first read the chapter. It is important. If they have to pee and have trouble getting their pants down, they will lose a few vital seconds. You want your child to practice actually pushing their pants down when *it's not a crisis— in moments when they don't actually* need to use the potty so the skill is in place when they do.

Be sure they're in very loose elastic-waist pants or shorts or leggings. For girls, dresses with no panties work great. For boys, boxers are pretty magical, but make sure he is commando. This means he's wearing boxers and only boxers, not boxers as undies. The idea behind this is that they need as little fabric on the bum as possible. I know we talked about this already, but it's worth repeating.

THE HALF AND HALF

Often parents are not really sure where their kid is with regard to taking everything in during the early phases of potty training. If you fall into this category, it's okay to do a day or two more of naked time. To make progress, though, we need to start stacking up successes to build your child's pride and confidence. Learning to use the potty is a lot like learning to read. You can't just learn a letter and move on. You have to study the letter, hear it again and again, and write it in lower- and uppercase many, many times. (I have a small rain forest in worksheets that prove this.) To create progress in potty training, you have to nudge the child forward with the expectation that they can rise to the next challenge, but you also have to know they've gotten the previous step. It's a balancing act, to be sure.

One way to hand your child success in block 2 is to do what I call "the half and half." It works like this. Start with your child naked (at least from the waist down), and make sure you get a good pee in the potty. Then throw on some clothes and maybe go for a very small outing (around the block or something similar). A change of scenery can also work wonders for both of you. Bracket the day's activities around pees, trying to ensure that you're home and your child has a naked bum for the times when they need to go. Between pees, put some pants on and do small errands or activities outside. This is handing the child success. They have no idea about the pride of not peeing in their pants, so we have to kind of hand it to them at first. Many parents feel like this is cheating, but it's not (or it is, and I don't care). The most valuable outcome here is that your child will feel pride and accomplishment. *These will provide the ongoing motivation.*

Between blocks 1 and 2, parents often try to rush things a bit. Get pants on the kid. Get out of the house. Get the kid fully potty trained. Part of the reason for clearing your social calendar is to be able to have a "whatever" attitude about the whole thing. If you rush, you'll be kicking out those blocks of success! They are vital. Without them, your tower is going to be unstable, if it stands at all. Take your time and set your child up to succeed.

Another thing: be sure *you* are taking care of yourself. Yes, this can be tiring. Make sure you're eating well and getting as much sleep as you can. This is a marathon, not a sprint. We need you sane and rested so you can be the most effective teacher possible.

THE FEELING OF HAVING TO GO PEE

Start using the phrase "the feeling of having to go pee" with your child. Some kids don't realize they need first to *feel it*, then make the move to the potty, then take their pants down, then sit and pee. Most kids respond best to short, direct commands. You don't have to bark this out like you're training a dog, but be short and direct and state things *in the order you would like them done*. This is vital. Potty training is the first thing your child is learning that has a set order with only one desirable outcome. That order can get mixed up, so make sure your kid is clear: Go. Pants. Sit. Pee.

Many kids hear you say, "Go pee!" and they do. It always reminds me of that old movie *Parenthood*, with Steve Martin. His daughter feels sick, and he says, "Honey, do you feel like you have to throw up?" And she says, "Okay," and pukes all over him. You want specific, short directions to indicate what they should be doing.

Let's look at other versions of the peeing through pants. Sometimes it's just that your child hasn't nailed that first block of learning. They should be able to pee on the potty when prompted or on their own while naked. If they can't or won't do that, you should hold off on the pants. Don't try to rush pants, and don't think of wearing pants as a marker of success. It's simply the next block of learning. We can't stack the "pants block" until we get the "naked block" down. Now you don't want a potty-trained-when-naked kid, so with some kids, you will need to nudge the process along. If you are unsure of what to do, try pants. If the pants get wet, "hand your child success" with the half and half.

If you think your child is trying to get to the potty but just isn't making it, keep going. Trying but not making it in time is a really good sign! If they are wetting through a few pairs of pants but you still feel pretty hopeful, keep going. I've had many parents echo what my former client Amy said:

> I just wanted to offer hope to those who may be feeling un-successful. The first couple of days resulted in many accidents. My daughter Katherine (twenty-two months) would start to pee on the floor, stop when I told her to hold it, not pee on the pot, and then have an accident right afterwards. Day two resulted in nine pairs of pants in seven hours (and two bare-bottomed accidents, as Kat liked being naked). The thing that helped me the most after the first couple of days was reading your blog entry about how parents have to be committed to this and not think that she wasn't ready yet and to wait a few more months. This morning I had a renewed resolve that this was it. I reminded Kat that she's a big girl now and doesn't use diapers anymore (except for sleeping, but I didn't remind her of that). She's acting like a big girl at mealtimes, too, not wanting to wear a bib and wanting to use grown-up utensils and plates! This has only been since potty training. She's been nursing more often today, but I think all the big girl responsibility is getting to her. I have to remind myself not to call her my baby. I just wanted to say thank you, Jamie! And I'm so glad I stuck it out!

Wet pants can be part of the learning process, but with all things, don't let it get out of control. I'd give it a day or two, and if pants are still being peed in, go back to block 1. Otherwise, your child is just practicing peeing in their pants and creating a new habit. Overall, if the child is not getting pee in the potty, what you should be looking for are these signs:

Distaste: They should feel yucky and it should register.
Apologetic: Any version of sorry.
Dismay: They are bothered that this happened.
Hiding: They are trying to hide it from you (this can also be flat-out denial that they peed their pants).

Any of those signs show that your child is aware of and has negative feelings about peeing their pants. This is when you would use the half-naked/half-clothed technique. They probably need a tiny bit more learning and a bit more confidence in their own abilities.

If your child pees their pants and registers nothing at all, it's time for at least one more naked day.

Still No Poop

So you're on block 2, and you still haven't gotten a poop. Your child may be showing signs of discomfort or crankiness, or both. Keep your eyes peeled because a poop will come eventually. *Be watchful when transitioning into pants if you don't have a poop yet.* The illusion of privacy that pants provide is a cue for them to just do it in their pants. I'll be warning you about this throughout the rest of this book. Pooping in pants can be one-off accidents for sure, but this becomes a new habit so fast that it's crazy. Don't let pooping in the pants become a regular thing. More about this in chapter 10, "Poop."

Even on the second day, no poop is very common. It's okay; don't panic. One of the biggest problems with lack of poop is that you start to get anxious. You also start hovering and slip into over-prompting.

Full-Blown Tantrums

Tantrums are not unheard of in a two-year-old who is not getting their way. In this particular case, "their way" is a diaper/routine/ everything back the way it was. Here's the thing with tantrums: they aren't very satisfying for your child if you aren't tugging at the other end of the proverbial rope. Here's a typical potty training tantrum situation. You prompt them to go pee on the potty. As you are making your way over to them, they suddenly throw themselves down on the floor, immediately becoming either super rigid or wet spaghetti-ish, they start screaming if you touch them, and . . . you know the rest. Here's the fix: the throw-away prompt, as in "remind and then walk away." The only reason a child would put on a show is that you are watching, front and center. If you prompt, leave it at that, and *really* walk away. It sounds risky, but you are giving them space and time to make a good decision for themselves. If a child is busy fighting you, all their energy is being used in fighting you rather than in making a good decision. So prompt and walk away. Never does a child have a tantrum in an empty room. The nature of the beast is that someone must be watching. Another trick if the child is not completely hysterical is to give a choice: "You can go pee now, or I can take off your pants so you can go on by yourself." Sometimes if you think they have to pee, it's just best to take those pants down without even giving them a choice. Doing that is in and of itself the reminder.

The Bedtime Potty Pit

In the game Candy Land, there are pits like the gooey Molasses Swamp that you can get stuck in. In potty training, there's a classic one I call the Bedtime Potty Pit (BPP). It can occur at two possible times: before giving up nighttime diapers and after giving up nighttime diapers. For brevity, I'll refer to nighttime only, but the same applies for naptime.

It looks something like this. Aaron does great all day long. His mom, Angela, can now trust him to use the potty during the day. He either tells her he has to go or does a really clear pee-pee dance. Daytime is all set. Aaron's bedtime is 7:30. There are the usual three stories and two songs. Dad's in charge of brushing teeth and PJs. Everything looks pretty good, almost out of a Lifetime movie. Then Aaron says, "I have to pee." Okay. PJs off, night diaper off, Aaron sits to pee. Shockingly, there's no pee. Diaper back on. PJs back on. Tuck Aaron in . . . almost out of the room, "Pee! I got to pee!" PJs off. Diaper off. Sit to pee. Hmm. No pee. You can rinse, lather, and repeat for however many times you can imagine. Even better is the poop call, because that just might lead to, let's say, forty minutes of reading to Aaron on the potty all for a poop.

It's classic—and freaking exhausting. Now, it's 8:30 and well past bedtime, which makes for the most charming behavior. But what do you do? Do you honor the pee and poop call? You've done all this hard work. What if he means it? But what if he doesn't?

My experience is that the BPP is a fabulous stall. Aaron has Mom and Dad wrapped around the idea of pottying and he knows it. Never in his short life has Aaron had the kind of power he has now. Mom and Dad jump when he says he has to pee. Aaron is not dumb; in fact, he's very smart. He's going to use that power as much as possible, largely for entertainment or to stall bedtime or both.

If you're caught in the BPP, give your child three chances (or however many you have predetermined). Let your child know that they have a certain number of chances. You might say something like, "Aaron, this is the last time you will sit to pee. If you don't have to pee, you can hold it until Mommy comes and gets you in the morning." He may or may not pee. You don't want to say, "Last chance, or you're stuck doing it in your diaper." At least introduce the notion that he can hold it and that it is up to him. He has a choice: A or B.

The other thing you should do if it looks like your child might use the BPP stall is to start bedtime early enough to factor it in. For Aaron, that might mean starting the whole bedtime routine around 6:45. Remember, this is temporary! You will all find your groove soon enough. If you build in time for the stall, you will be much less likely to get anxious about it. The stalls are annoying enough on their own, but in addition, we get anxious because bedtime is being put off, and we know the kid needs his sleep or we're stuck with the fallout the next day. So allow yourself plenty of wiggle room.

Don't be afraid of laying down some firm boundaries. Once he has nothing to push against, the game really isn't fun. As always, do this in a calm, casual manner. Even if he calls out one last time to pee as you're leaving the room, you can say, "Okay, hold it till morning. I love you. Good night." This way, you've acknowledged that you've heard him and that you believe him (even if you don't), but you laid down some boundaries and you're sticking to them. This is good parenting.

And you don't have to be concerned if he does pee in his diaper; it's not going to screw with the process. It's a minor behavioral speed bump. Deal with the stall game first, then tackle the nighttime potty training. Do *not* tell him to "just go in your diaper." Even though we're not caring if he DOES, we don't want to specifically say to do that.

Of course, this all gets much trickier without a nighttime diaper, because you have the very real fear that your kid will pee the bed. You never want to lead with fear! The best thing to do is leave the potty chair in their room and after the bedtime routine say, "Good night. I love you. If you need to pee, your potty is right there." If your child senses you are fearful and unsure, I can guarantee this will become a game for them.

One really great trick is to include a double pee in the nighttime routine. I also find a small whiteboard with all the things included in the routine. Yes, I realize they're most likely not reading yet but this is a nice visual cue and fun for them to cross off. No one gaslights more than a kid stalling at bedtime. They'll say you didn't sing the song you just did or that you only read two stories when you actually read three. The whiteboard gives the proof. I know you're tired and susceptible to all the nonsense. It also makes it distracting to slip in that double pee. That might look like: Time to get ready for bed. Put on PJs and pee. Brush teeth, read stories, last pee, sing songs, and whatever else you may do.

If you keep running into this, check in with your connection time with your child, particularly if they're in full-time day care. Most kids fully decompress only as bedtime rolls around. Stalling bedtime is not just a pain-in-the-ass manipulation; it's a bid for more connection time. Be sure to truly connect with your little one, even in the rushed hours of getting home, dinner, bedtime, and so on. A great way to connect is "roses and thorns" (some people call this highs and lows). You go over the best parts of the day and the worst parts. It serves as a great check-in and connecting point at the end of the day.

Power Struggles

Another huge issue involved in potty training troubles is the power struggle. This is most certainly the age of power struggles, and they can make things a little crazy in your house. The average family deals with several power struggles on a daily basis, so potty training power struggles should come as no surprise. Still, it's best to avoid them if possible, which is why it's so important to avoid hovering or overprompting. Both lead to power struggles.

Should you find yourself facing a power struggle, you need to identify and remove whatever is creating it. This is because you cannot and will not ever win a power struggle with a toddler. I had a classic one with Pascal. He was about two feet away from me, and I asked him to come over to me in a casual tone. He responded, "No, you come here." I followed with, "No, you come here." We kept going back and forth, and as I started digging in my heels, so did he. Finally, I was able to put on my grown-up brain for a minute and realize we were in a fight *about two feet of space*, and I didn't even really need him to come to me! Jeez Louise! Come on, Mommy.

Don't even try to tell me that something similar hasn't happened to you. So as you can imagine, if power struggles can erupt over nothing, think of the power struggle potential of something as big and loaded as potty training. It's a natural hotbed for a struggle.

Also, unlike other potential causes of power struggles, when it comes to potty training, your child truly does hold THE POWER, in a very literal way. We sometimes feel as if our whole world revolves around and is controlled by our kids. The reality, though, is they have no control at all. We tell them where, when, why, and how to do practically everything. This is normal. Their bodily functions, though, are one thing we don't control! They hold the pee (or poop), so they hold the power.

If we look at a power struggle as a tug-of-war, the absolute best way out of one is to let go of your end of the rope. This does not mean you cave in to what your child wants; it means you let go of your need to control the situation. Most often with toddlers, power struggles arise out of a desire to "do it myself." This is true of potty training as well. Whenever you find yourself engaged in a potty training power struggle, the way you let go of your end of the rope is to allow your child to make using the potty his idea. For instance, you could use one of those throwaway prompts I have noted in previous chapters. Prompt and back off. You do not want to hammer home your point or keep repeating the same thing again and again. It won't work, and things will escalate.

Too Much Talking

Yes; talking to your child is good. And yes, telling your child what you are doing as you are doing it is good. But like all things, talking is good in moderation. There's a current parenting trend that seems to favor a little *too* much talking. Some parents want to explain every little thing, giving a mini-dissertation about everything that happens. Some of this, I think, comes from us trying too hard to "actively teach." Also, some of it—particularly when it comes to potty training—is to mask our own fear.

Here's the thing: as long as you are talking, you are not listening. Also, as long as you are talking, you are not letting your child talk to himself. Self-talk is crucial to language and thought development. It is what helps your child learn to control their impulses. Self-talk develops along with your child and becomes their inner voice. Some experts suggest that children who develop strong self-talk skills make better choices throughout childhood. We may be talking about pee and poop right now, but eventually it's going to be smoking and drugs and sex. With the constant barrage of noise around us in modern society, adding our own voices to the cacophony is not always helpful. When your child talks to themselves, they're sorting out all the information they take in and making it their own. They're learning to make good decisions *for themselves*. If you are talking, this can't happen.

Furthermore, when you're talking to your child—about potty training or anything else—you're generally also worrying about things along the lines of: "Is he even listening? Or comprehending?" This adds another layer to the talking problem. There's emotion under all that talking. With regard to potty training, that emotion is most likely fear and anxiety (on your part). Children attend to your vibe far above your words.

The bottom line is that most parents talk endlessly to their children about the steps involved in potty training. And most of the time, the kid can recite those steps right back to you. If your child can tell you where the pee and poop go but they are still peeing on the floor, it's time to stop talking. Instead, use simple directives without a lot of explanation. Then be quiet to give your child room to process the information for themselves.

Having Trouble with Releasing or Hating the Potty?

THE RED SOLO CUP TRICK

The Red Solo Cup trick, made famous by country music and drinking college students everywhere, comes to the rescue. It is oh-so-much-more than an unbreakable drinking container. It is also a most excellent Insta-Porta-Potty.

Now, first off, it doesn't have to be red or Solo brand. Any wide-mouth, deep container will do. And clearly this is a better trick for boys but can work surprisingly well for girls too.

I personally discovered the RSC idea because I have one bathroom. Invariably—and I do mean always—the minute I would sit to pee, my son would announce that he also had to pee. He was well beyond the little potty stage by this time, so I started keeping an RSC under the sink, tucked away so guests didn't ask questions and no one could mistake it for a drinking vessel.

Here are just a few additional ideas for the Red Solo Cup:

- In the early stages of potty training, the cup is great if your child needs some "switching up"; sometimes they start resisting the potty just because they're sick of all the hoopla around it.
- The RSC is good if you have a child who's having trouble relaxing and releasing the pee. The cup allows them to focus only on releasing rather than having to worry about sitting too.
- It is easy to keep a cup in every room for emergencies. Remember that at first, you only have a few seconds' warning to get to the potty.
- If your child is resistant to leaving the activity they're immersed in, you can offer the cup as a choice.
- If your child is in the tub and announces they have to pee, have the cup handy. It's perfectly fine for your child to pee in the tub, but if they're asking, it's best to honor the request and respond. The RSC lets you avoid the whole soaking-wet transfer to the potty and back to the tub (which usually creates so much commotion that they can't relax and release the pee once they're on the toilet anyway).
- The RSC is handy to keep in the car for a quick pee before arriving at or after leaving from somewhere. (Do yourself a *huge favor* and keep a mason jar with a lid in

the car just in case. At the beach or lake or in a snowsuit, it's easy to pull out and let your kid do their business with hardly anyone noticing. Sometimes for kids who are just not loving the potty, the RSC is simply more fun.

A lot of parents balk at the idea of having their kid pee in a cup. A lot of parents also find out that this is a great trick and soon start worrying that their child will *only* ever pee in a cup. The RSC trick is a temporary bridge to using the potty. I have *never* come across a child who stuck with the trick for a weird period of time.

The Hover within the Prompt

Check in on your prompting: Are you overprompting? Can you back off? You may feel confident that you are not overprompting, but you are still seeing some resistance to your occasional prompts. What's probably happening is that you are hovering after prompting. You may be prompting your child and then standing there, waiting or physically taking them to the potty (depending on their age, you may need to do this, but if they're older than twenty-four months, you don't) and watching over them to make sure they sit and pee. The trick is to prompt or remind and then *walk away* (just as you do when you're facing a tantrum). It can feel risky, but you have to leave room for them to make the call. Think of the prompt as a reminder, not as a "make them go" kind of thing. There is nothing for them to resist if you act as if you don't care. It's a balance of still being there to help but also letting them claim this as their own. I won't stop repeating this: *the thing that really moves potty training along is pride in self-mastery.*

Blocks 2 and 3 are the heart of potty training. You should be feeling a sense of progress, even if it's teeny-tiny. There may be a day or two during these blocks when it looks as if you've stalled out or even gone a little backward. That's okay. Very little learning in any area is linear; it's almost always a cha-cha. However, if you are seeing no progress at all, hang in there a few more days. Blocks 2 and 3 tend to coincide with the first few days of potty training. I like to give it at least five to seven days before giving up. Legions of parents are completely hopeless the first few days and suddenly, on day 5, everything clicks into place. It's always shocking to me how little time we give our kids to learn this milestone. We don't do this with ANY other milestone.

CHAPTER 9

Block 4 and All the Rest

This chapter is about all the weird little things that can come up late in potty training or after potty training. You never know when some of these might hit, so I'm lumping them all here.

Public Restrooms

The first thing to keep in mind is your attitude about public restrooms. If you are all strung out about them touching anything in them, you will freak out your little one. It's also important to bear in mind that most kids have a really hard time with public restrooms. They are "live," meaning the tile and steel and porcelain bounce sound around. In addition, there's usually a hand dryer going off without warning, and all that noise may be too much for them. In the beginning, it's best to choose a single-room family bathroom if possible. You can also carry a travel potty or just a little potty for the back of the car to avoid public restrooms altogether. If that's not possible, I recommend foldable inserts. These are the little toilet seat reducers and they fold into quarters. You can easily keep one in a baggie.

Another great trick is to have concert headphones or earmuffs in your bag. Your child can wear these if the noise bothers them. I highly suggest carrying sticky notes as well to block the automatic flusher. If that goes off and the toilet flushes, your child will lose it. Most of all, stay as chill as you can and you'll have better success. Our nonverbal communication is everything here.

Little (or Bigger) Backsliding

This applies if you have a kid who was doing great with the potty and then started having accidents, seemingly out of the blue. This also applies if your child has done fine and suddenly starts to dribble, meaning a little pee lands in their undies or pants, but they don't have a full accident. In some cases this seems like it becomes the actual cue to go to the bathroom.

Accidents come out of the blue.

First and foremost, remember that you can't suddenly unlearn something. I've had parents say, "He was totally potty trained for a few months and then started having accidents at preschool. I guess he's capable but just not ready." Guys. That makes no sense. If you learn something and backslide, something is amiss; it has nothing to do with not being ready. The first thing to do is go back to block 1, even if they're in day care; you can do this on the weekend. Sometimes things get all jangled in their little minds. It could just be a small refresher. You don't have to watch them like you did in the beginning. But we need to see if they can handle it with zero obstacles (like pants).

- Try to see a pattern, which is a good practice in all of potty training. Are the accidents only at school? Only at home? Only while out and about? Or is it across the board all the time?

- School/day care is fun but also very distracting. Maybe the child needs to go back to being reminded. Has anything changed there—teachers, classrooms, friends? We'll talk a lot more about this in chapter 12, "Day Care Struggles."

- When did your little one last poop? They are tiny inside and even a couple of days of not pooping can lead to pressure on the bladder, causing accidents.

- Any big life changes: New sibling? A move? A divorce? A major sickness or injury? All of these can throw a kid off track. Again, the solution is to run through all the blocks again.

Are the accidents what you'd consider to be "cluster accidents": they seem to go for a couple of days or weeks with no problem, then have two days of consistent waterworks? Cluster accidents are a sign of a poop blockage, which we fully cover in chapter 10, "Poop." But for now, a poop blockage can be present even if the child seems to be pooping plenty.

Sometimes the issue may seem to be one thing, but when you start following the trail, you realize it's something else. I'll use the example of my own son. He was fully trained and then suddenly started having a couple of nighttime accidents a week. At that point, I wasn't even monitoring his fluid intake before bed. He'd wake up to pee if he had to. So this was odd, and I started watching him carefully. I eventually figured out the accidents stemmed from the fact that he had switched day cares. The switch wasn't a big deal to him, but the new day care was more structured than his previous one. The kids drank fluids only at snack or mealtime, and even then, using only a Dixie cup. My son didn't know he could ask for more. Instead, he came home and downed five huge glasses of water. Even potty training all-stars can't handle that kind of fluid intake so late in the day. Once I told him he could ask for water at day care whenever he was thirsty, he came home and drank a normal amount, and the problem was solved. I thought it would be obvious to him to ask for more if he was thirsty, but it wasn't. (Funny enough, he has no problem demanding more at home.) So what I could have maybe assumed was some emotional adjustments to a new day care was really strategizing consistent fluid consumptions.

Dribbles

We talked a bit about dribbles that happen in the early days of potty training. These are different dribbles. It doesn't happen to all kids but when it does, it's usually quite a few months after potty training. This is almost always the child experimenting with how long they can hold their pee. A key thing to remember is that letting out a little pee and stopping the flow takes an enormous amount of control, so this isn't a backslide and it isn't an accident.

I define a dribble as a half-dollar size or less of pee. If your child is starting to do this, do not call them accidents and do not make a big deal about them. Simply keep reminding them that they need to go to the potty when they *have the feeling to go pee.* If you continually make a big deal or call it an accident, they can totally throw in the towel and start to not care anymore. If it's a half accident or more, again, go back to pantsless for a half or whole day and refresh the process. One accident is just that: unintentional and truly an accident. In my work, it's not a thing until it's happened three or more times. Just keep that in mind.

One final thought on accidents: do not put a diaper back on your child! Once they are potty training, even in the beginning stages, putting a diaper on your child says one thing and one thing only: "I don't trust you. I'm telling you all day that I know you can do it, and I have confidence in you. But, really, I don't trust you." This is extremely damaging to the whole process. If you don't trust your child, they will never trust themselves. (They may have to go back to a diaper if they're in day care, but we'll talk about that in chapter 12, "Day Care Struggles.")

Should your child have an accident, don't punish or berate them. Have them help you clean it up, and reassure them that you know they can make it to the potty next time. Of course, this is for the occasional accident. Severe regressions indicate a big problem that I address in chapter 16, "Special Circumstances, including Delays and Neurodiversity."

They Get It, They Lose It; They Get It, They Lose It

Once your child has had a couple of successes in a row, you know they can do it. The learning process is over. Yes, there can still be accidents, but there will generally be some clear reason for them. If there isn't, head over to chapter 13, "Behavior versus Potty Training," and give the ideas presented there some thought.

Once your child starts to use the potty correctly, you know they *can*. Again, try to find a pattern. Sometimes this occurs from what I called "lazy learning," although I must be abundantly clear: I know of zero lazy toddlers. But occasionally accidents start happening at home when we are doing too much for a child, not letting them do for themselves or have any responsibility. Children rise to our expectations, so be sure to let them take over some responsibility overall, which will help them not think you'll do the work of pottying them.

Pooping in Nap/Night Diaper

So you're a couple of weeks into potty training, and it's coming to your attention that your child is saving poop for the nap or nighttime diaper. The first thing to ascertain is whether they are specifically holding it in for those times or they appear to have adjusted their body clock. If they are holding it (a version of withholding), they clearly have to go poop but won't want to sit to release. Or they actually ask to go for a nap when it's nowhere near naptime. Another tell is if they poop the *minute* you put on the diaper, while they are awake. If they're pooping while asleep, they might have switched their body clock OR they may just really relax and their body relaxes and just lets go. Here are some tips for both of these situations:

- If they are obviously withholding and you're seeing escalating and panicky behavior, go to chapter 10, "Poop," and also the Don't Panic section at the end of the book.
- If you're in the first few weeks of potty training and it's not obvious withholding, I'd give it some time to shake out. Many times this resolves on its own as your little one gets comfortable with pottying in the waking hours.
- Night and nap train. Many kids consciously or unconsciously hold out for the diaper. When they have no diaper option, a good percentage of them just start pooping in the potty—or they are actually withholders and you can see that clearly. Revisit the "Nighttime Training" and "Poop" chapters.
- Let it go. If you don't want to night train and your child is not in distress from withholding, just clear your plate of this worry. Diapers are for one thing and one thing only: to contain pee and poop. You cannot use one and simultaneously not expect your child to not use it for its intended use. So know your capacity at this time and let it go until you can change things.

Revenge Pee or Just High Emotions

Let's say your child has done something wrong and they've been sent to a time-out. (I don't love time-outs but I realize many people use them. My other book, *Oh Crap! I Have a Toddler*, is based on no time-outs.) Once there, they pee all over the place. If emotions are super-high, chances are, whether it's due to a reprimand or just a meltdown, most kids will pee themselves. I do not recommend time-outs in general, and particularly during potty training, because of this.

Sometimes it's unclear whether it's a high-emotion accident or a more purposeful eff you. Generally, fixing wonky behavior like feeling that you're getting an eff you is about more connection with your child. I will say that connection HAS to happen before correction, so bear that in mind no matter what.

"The Inner 'F**k It'"

If you have been going at potty training for a few weeks and you are still getting one or more accidents a day consistently, it's time to go back and do block 1 over again. A child having that many accidents doesn't really count as being potty trained. What most likely happened is that something went wrong somewhere along the way, and your child has a gap in their understanding. You don't have to go through the whole process again, but be sure to cover the basics.

The problem is this: if a child has a gap in their learning or understanding, they will quickly transition their attitude into what I call "the inner 'f**k it.'" This is the "I don't care" attitude that comes from being stuck and not knowing how to get out of it. Think of the punk in high school who talked back and skipped classes. Nine times out of ten that kid had a learning disorder or other circumstances that interfered with their ability to succeed. The attitude was just a front. The same thing can happen with potty training. We humans like to be good at what we attempt. When we can't do something well, we tend to pretend we don't care about it. Of course, this isn't a logical or conscious thought process, but it's what's going on. Go back and breeze through blocks 1, 2, and 3 with your child, and figure out where the gap in learning is. (I'm betting it's between being naked and wearing clothes.)

Wiping

And the most frequently asked question of all time: When will this kid wipe their own butt?

Butt wiping typically takes a while. Most kids don't even begin to do a good job until they are about five or maybe six years old. Often this is just about logistics. Their arms are just not long enough to reach around and do a good job. You can begin to teach this like you teach brushing teeth. You let them have a turn, and then you're the real cleanup crew. I know a lot of preschools and camps demand fully potty trained, including wiping their own butts. While I understand this, I also think it's completely unrealistic. If this is your situation, just do your best with your child and expect skid marks from not-the-best job.

Those are most of the major snafus that can arise in your first month or so of potty training. There's still a lot more information about these yet to come in this book. It's a bit tricky because these problems don't always occur at the same point for every kid, so you might be looking for an answer and it's not where you think it might be. Keep reading and don't forget about the index and chapter 17, "Random Tips and Questions."

CHAPTER 10

Poop

All we have done as mothers, fathers, and humans—graduate school, careers, global travel, making art, making life—culminates in being brought to our knees because our child did or did not poop in the potty. Had someone told you five years ago that you'd be here now, you'd probably have laughed out loud. But here it is. Poop. The begging. The cajoling. The eagle eye for signals. If you have cried over poop, this chapter is for you.

You are not the first, and will not be the last, to have poop on the brain. Poop is an endless topic in potty training—everything from slight, unconscious withholding, to willful pooping on the floor, to massive power struggles over requesting a diaper in which to poop. So poop makes up an entire chapter of this book, and in it, we're going to delve into a lot of things: society, philosophy, mythology and, yes, actual crap. To make sense of poop, you need to think about your child's perspective and see this through their eyes. There are a few things to keep in mind.

First, all your child has ever known is the feeling of squishy, warm poop right up against their little bums. Second, as they see it, no one has ever paid much attention to this very primal, very private function before today. Third, pooping while standing up or

161

squatting is far more natural than pooping while sitting. Fourth, going from pooping in a diaper to pooping in a potty can be freaky as hell. Your patience is required. Your child has no notion yet of the beauty of a clean bum. It's okay; they'll get there.

Think about your own poop. You know those gigunda poops? The ones that make you feel like you lost five pounds in one sitting? Personally I love those poops, but imagine how they feel to a small child. It must feel like all their insides are falling out. Of course, they've been pooping all along, but the free-drop into the potty can be disconcerting. Poops can be scary. To make them a little less so, I encourage parents to let their children empty their own small pot into the big toilet. When you do this, you're going to crack up (or be really grossed out): almost all kids are fascinated by their poop. They will carry that pot to the big toilet staring and smelling and checking out everything about that poop, mostly with a ton of pride: "I did THAT? THAT came outta MY butt? Cooool."

Pooping issues are usually one of two things: holding it in or letting it out (at the wrong time, in the wrong place). Unfortunately, the more the child holds it in, the more likely it is to come out at the wrong time.

So let's take a minute to dissect the modern poop situation. I'm here to tell you that pooping has gotten more problematic over the past several decades. If your mom wants to tell you about how easy it was for her to get you to poop on the potty, fine. That was then, this is now. We are living in a different world, and we are different parents. I've been potty training kids since 2002. I wrote the first edition of this book in 2009 and started helping massive numbers of people in 2011. Pooping has become more of a problem lately. I know this.

Also, I'm fascinated with why things have changed so drastically in one generation. Pooping is not only thought of as such a big ordeal, but is becoming even more troublesome with each passing year. So I've spent an inordinate amount of time dissecting the poop problem. I will be sharing only the highlights because *no one* wants to hear everything I have to say about poop.

Sir Thomas Crapper

This guy is credited with inventing the flushing toilet in the 1800s. He was a plumber and eventually bought the patent. The real inventor was Sir John Harington, who invented his first toilet in 1596. Still, that's pretty useless information, and I'm sticking with Sir Crapper as the dude who invented the potty. It just sounds better. Anyway, the toilet has been around for a pretty long while. I've traveled the globe and have been in countries where squatting and squat toilets are the norm. Let me tell you: squatting is a better way to poop. It turns out there's a reason for this. The anorectal angle (the angle of the tunnel that carries your poop to your anus) gets kinked up upon sitting. When you're squatting or standing, though, there's no kinking. This makes evacuation more than easy; it's almost effortless (and toilet-paper-less).

I believe the fact that we (culturally) sit to poop is part of the problem with kids and pooping, particularly with our bodies at a ninety degree angle. We adults have grown very used to it and can deal with it, but for kids, the transition from squatting or standing to poop (which they often do when wearing a diaper) to sitting is highlighted during potty training. By itself, though, this doesn't fully explain the Big Poop Problem. Some kids have no trouble sitting and pooping, and the toilet has been around for a long time. If the sitting position were the sole cause of pooping problems, we would've ditched it long before now.

Still, sitting contributes to poop trouble, so until the perfect potty chair is designed—I'm working on it—when your child sits to poop, you can put some books underneath their feet to bring their thighs close to the chest. This helps create proper anorectal alignment and makes pooping infinitely easier. I personally use a Squatty Potty. You might consider this for yourself and for your child as they get bigger; Pascal was six when we started using it and he loved it. Now that he's seventeen, I don't ask what happens in the bathroom.

In short, the proper poop position is important, but it can't be the sole reason for pooping problems.

Pooping Is Primal

Pooping itself is a very primal function. Our poop is a piece of us—literally—and releasing it requires privacy, which a diaper affords. When a child's bum is covered, it feels concealed and private. It's keeping the bum out in the air, which we do when we potty train, that makes pooping feel public and uncomfortable at first. As adults, we usually go to a small room dedicated to pooping and close the door. We don't take kindly to intruders. Our children have those same desires. If your child resists pooping, the first thing you should offer is privacy, with the level of privacy you can give depending on the age of the child. Age also tends to determine how much privacy your child needs. Kids under the age of twenty-four months generally need less. From twenty-four months on, each passing month will bring your child more self-awareness, which usually means they need more privacy. Offering your child privacy can be as simple as "forgetting" something in the other room once your child is situated on the potty. Alternately, you can close the bathroom door. Simply put, too often, especially during potty training, there's a glaring spotlight on a very personal function. But again, that's just one little piece of the pooping puzzle.

Your Poop Values

Poop values is a term I made up to describe your family's view on poop. Do you like poop? Is pooping a joke in your house? (It's better if it is.) When someone goes into the bathroom and leaves a big stink behind, do you talk about the elephant in the room, or do you just not say anything? Are you the sort of family who, when someone farts, everyone pretends it didn't happen? Are you the kind of person who can only poop at home? Simply put, are you embarrassed by poop, or is it just one of those things?

In general, we are a culture that disdains poop. Attitudes aside, though, it's a vital bodily function that allows us to eliminate the waste products of our digestion. I've heard it said, "You aren't what you eat. You are what you don't shit."

Your poop values are going to be passed on to your child. If you don't like poop, your child won't either. If you think it's the most disgusting thing in the world, so will your child. If you can poop only at home, chances are your kid will be the same way. None of that is intended as judgment. It's just fact. Some parents are weird about poop, but they expect their child to poop on a potty sitting in the middle of the living room.

I suggest that before beginning potty training, you make it a point to have your child in the bathroom with you while you poop. This is the best way to model the potty behavior you're going to be teaching. Your child can see that pooping sometimes might take several minutes and that people sometimes grunt or make facial expressions. And they see that poop falls out of you, into the toilet, and nobody dies because of it. These are all very valid reasons to have your child see you poop. You don't have to have them with you every time. In fact, it's just as valuable to once in a while announce that you have to go poop and you'd like some privacy. This is a good way to introduce this word and notion.

Diet

We can't look at pooping problems without talking about diet. Most kids have a pretty good diet when they're young (I'll say up to about twenty-four months). Most parents focus on fruits, veggies, and other good stuff. Most parents allow the occasional treat or juice box. After their child turns two, though, I find that most parents start caving in a little more. The number of birthday party invitations increases and, along with them, treat consumption increases. Parents start allowing a little more candy or juice or whatever the case may be. It is, in general, something we all start to relent on a little bit more.

Two years of age is also around the time that toddlers can start to get picky. They start showing food preferences, and it's usually crappy food they prefer. This is the age when the "won't eat anything but macaroni and cheese" phase begins. This is also the age of on-the-go food. Your child has probably mastered eating without you watching every bite to make sure they don't choke, right? So you're more comfortable giving snacks in the car and at the playground. These snacks, like crackers and dry cereal, are generally easy to grab and not horribly messy.

This isn't a nutrition book, but I'd be remiss if I didn't include a bit about food and how it affects potty training. Certain foods irritate the bladder and can cause lots of little accidents. Other foods can cause uncontrollable poop. But there's a huge looming problem that has begun to rear its head in the past decade: food that's too soft, especially pouches, puffs, and baked goods. Here's a quick recap of digestion. It begins in the brain and the eyes with seeing and smelling food. Next comes the mouth, and here's where it gets really interesting. Chewing food well releases digestive enzymes that start the whole digestive process. If we don't chew hard and long, those enzymes don't get released, which totally messes with digestion. In addition, refined and processed foods, especially carbohydrates, inhibit peristalsis, the pulsing motion that moves food through the GI tract. As busy as we are as parents, we should try to have food that needs good chewing, with sit-down meals as much as possible. At this age, food doesn't have to be fancy, but it's good to keep it as unprocessed as possible.

I also have to mention food allergies and sensitivities here in the poop section. One in three of my clients with poop problems end up with a food allergy sensitivity diagnosis. Gluten is the major offender, with dairy being a close second. *If your child is either often constipated or has loose stools*, do yourself a huge favor and start experimenting. *If your child is pooping loose stools more than four times a day,* something is not right. More important, your child is not digesting their food, which can lead to malnutrition.

I know food allergies are a major pain in the butt. But when parents realize a food culprit and fix it, their child's poop problem miraculously is gone. I once worked with a little boy who would have some uncontrollable poops. It wasn't diarrhea, and it wasn't all the time so his parents couldn't figure it out. It turns out this kid couldn't even have the tiniest amount of chocolate or citrus, even as flavorings. It's worth noting that this child saw an allergist and wasn't deemed allergic to either of these. In my experience, allergy testing is sometimes great but often doesn't pick up on sensitivities causing poop problems so you may have to start experimenting and being vigilant.

And now a few words about fat. The low-fat craze is no good, especially for young children. Be sure your child is getting adequate, healthy fats. Good sources are coconut oil, avocado, olive oil, high-quality butter, and animal fat like tallow. Adequate fat will not only help with pooping, but it seems that it improves a child's ability to focus and behave as it levels off blood sugar.

I eat an ancestral diet (formerly called paleo) and I've never experienced such health as I do now. I don't eat grains and don't feed them to my son. When I switched his way of eating, he became, I swear to God, nearly angelic in behavior. He is also much more focused throughout the day and is not constantly hungry. His bleeding eczema is gone. I'm only mentioning this because food is our fuel and what goes in has everything to do with how it comes out.

If your child is having a hard time with pooping, you may be tempted to up their fiber level. Over the years, I've found that this backfires. Certainly a bit of fiber is fine, but adding some or becoming focused on tons of fiber can backfire. We can't make a kid drink a ton of water, and too much fiber can back up the poop to the point of difficulty. I've found that coconut in any form—oil, flakes, or milk—to be the *best* for loosening up poops. You can make recipes with coconut, but just a teaspoon or two of the milk or oil will move things along very nicely. The coconut milk should be full fat and the kind in a can, not a carton in the fridge. The latter is watered down too much and not effective for pooping purposes. Regardless, from my experience, I recommend increasing your child's fat consumption before upping their fiber. It makes that big a difference.

All this aside, even diet doesn't completely solve the pooping puzzle. The right diet certainly will help, but it's not the complete answer. After all, it's not like the day you start potty training your child completely changes their eating, right? And still, many parents with a child who pooped three times a day, no problem, with a diaper on, see drama start when the diaper comes off. So some of the trouble has got to be in the potty training.

The "Poop Problem" and Modern Life

Here's where things get interesting. I've looked at the poop problem from all angles and have found that for generations upon generations, pooping has generally not been a problem. Suddenly the last ten years are bringing about increasing poop problems. Diet is a factor. Squatting versus sitting is a factor. Still, there's one factor we haven't looked at, and in my opinion, it's the big one: the speed at which our world moves. These days, we get information and connect with others so much faster than previous generations ever did. I think the world is moving too damn fast for our kids, and as a result, they are anxious, regardless of how we try individually to combat this at home.

If we think of your child as fundamentally anxious and of the diaper as your child's oldest and dearest security blanket, the poop problem makes sense. In fact, I don't think it's the pooping *itself* that is the problem. I think our children are clinging to the literal security blanket of something (the diaper) that they've known since birth. Lately, I've seen more and more kids literally asking for a diaper to poop in as opposed to using the potty. Ten years ago, this was nearly unheard of, but now it's becoming increasingly common.

Let's go further and examine the psychology of withholding (not pooping) and its opposite, which is letting go (pooping). As far back as mythology, withholding versus letting go has been a common theme. Even today, that theme drives a lot of movie plots. So if pooping is the Grand Pooh-Bah of letting go, why would a child withhold?

This is an interesting question and worth examining. We as a society are on edge. Our politics are damn near a reality show. Social media has become an addiction. Online news, the ability to Like and Share, email—all of these things combine to make for a fast-paced world. And then to top it all off, we had COVID in 2020. And the world has most certainly not gotten any less anxious. We, as parents, but moms in particular, are subject to an onslaught of not only frightening news (e.g., kidnappings) but also parenting media drama. All this just serves to confuse us and wound our intuition. It also makes us feel anxious, which our children pick up on.

But media isn't the only factor. Children are now a market more so than ever before. That is another big difference I see in comparing a generation ago and now. Birthday parties are big events, and kids get invited to a lot of them. I met a mom who couldn't find a good weekend to start potty training her two-year-old; six weekends in a row were packed with back-to-back birthday parties. That's too much.

Many parents have written to ask me if their child can go to swim class or toddler gym or music class on the second day of potty training. Working potty training into your toddler's schedule is doing things in reverse order. Potty training is a vital life skill; your child needs to learn how to put poop in a potty more than they need to attend a music class. But that's neither here nor there. The point is that kids these days have busy schedules. We all know that overscheduling is not good, and we may not think of our toddlers as being truly overscheduled, but for toddlers, just about anything can count as a big event. I think our children are running on fumes most of the time and have what I call "emotional hangovers."

There's also the fact that parents are highly invested in "making memories." In my opinion, memories get made in the small, lovely moments that take place between you and your child. They don't necessarily require Disneyland or the latest Whatever-on-Ice. The bottom line is that we are moving too fast and are too overscheduled and that can affect pooping.

Now, I live in the real world, and I love social media and my smartphone, so I'm not suggesting you give up all media, but I am asking you to slow down. Try to combat the overt marketing to our children at home. Take time to revel in their milestones, like potty training, zippering up zippers, tying shoes, and riding bikes. Children love routine, and they need time to discover the world around them. Downtime is not only good; it's essential. Boredom begets creativity; it's good for the soul.

To return to our discussion of poop, I think our fast-paced world is largely responsible for poop problems and why they're so common. I hear from many moms, "I've been home with my kid for two whole days potty training. I'm going out of my mind." No offense, but spending two days at home shouldn't make you go crazy. Just something to think about.

Be sure you are creating a safe haven for your child, so they have room to slow down and explore at their own pace. We have it all backward today. We are overstimulating and overscheduling in one breath, and yet in the next, we are delaying life skill milestones (like potty training).

My son's preschool was fantastic. They were very Montessori/ Waldorfy but had no official affiliation with either. They baked their own snacks every day and sat family style. They poured their own water and measured stuff. No characters were allowed to encourage marketing to children, no sugar was allowed in their lunch boxes—that kind of school. One of the reasons I chose this school was because there was no play yard. The school was located downtown, and the kids used the city around them. They went out every day of the year—except for one very blizzardy day—in cold, rain, shine, or snow. I highly valued that.

They also taught the kids how to dress themselves completely for the weather. How to get on snow pants and mittens and boots.

How to zipper and button and tie. It was fantastic!! This teaching of life skills was so much more valuable than any other sort of "teaching" they could have done. We live in New England, and having a three-year-old who can get his own winter clothes on is truly amazing. I bring this up because to me, that's the right order of things. My child's brain didn't need specific stimulation for math or reading or music. My child needed to be in control of his own person. Learning life skills like how to use the potty lets that happen. It builds inherent self-pride in mastery. That's where self-esteem grows. (This school, the Dr. Pat Feinstein Childhood Development Center, is located in Providence, Rhode Island, and it's everything you want in a preschool.)

What to Do about the Pooping

All this chatter about why pooping has gotten harder is all well and good, but you're here because you want to know what to do about it, so let's look at the most common scenarios and some super special ones too. As we do so, something to keep in mind above all else is that this is *all new*. The feeling of warm, squishy poop next to your child's bum is the norm. A free-falling poop into "a pit" of sorts can be scary. It's our social norm to put our poop in a container, but remember that for the better part of two years, your *child's* norm has been the diaper.

There are many facets to why pooping is so dramatic that I've broken the topic down into digestible parts. Let's take a few minutes and look at the many things that could be going on. First, there is the slight unconscious withholding, a huge concern for a lot of parents. It might look like this: your child used to poop two or three times a day in a diaper. Now you officially start potty training and . . . no poop. There may be resistance to actually sitting on the potty. Some children will say a variation of "my bum hurts." Or they may say nothing, and there's just no poop. The trick here to remember is that poop is personal in a very primal way. We as adults understand that when it comes to ourselves, but somehow we forget it when it comes to kids. Poop is one of the few things we can truly call our own. Here's another way to look at it: it's said that the mouth and teeth are highly emotional, which is why so many people panic at a trip to the dentist. It's an orifice. It's mine. Don't go in there. Right? Well, that's an orifice everyone can see! The butthole was not meant for scrutiny. And yet, here we are all up in our kids' business and what they keep up there. This whole process was kept tucked away in a diaper. Of course, you did change the diaper, but you had no part in how the poop came out. You had no idea how the process worked for your kid. You probably saw a "poop face," but that's just when it got pushed out. We have no idea how long it took to "park itself on the off ramp." So now you start potty training and it's like this glaring spotlight has been put on your kid's butt and what it produces.

Let's take another minute to talk about that glaring spotlight on an otherwise private function. The anus is a sphincter muscle that opens and closes with emotion. (This is one of my favorite lines in this book. I'm even thinking of getting T-shirts made. Because I am not well.)

I'll give an example by way of another big sphincter muscle: the cervix, one of the major muscles responsible for a baby's journey into the world. Ina May Gaskin, a world-renowned midwife, explains how the cervix needs to be open to effectively give birth. She also notes that it can slam shut:

> Even when the voluntary muscles get tired, the sphincters don't get tired. Those are connected to the organs that fill up with something; the bladder, uterus, intestines. They expand and contract, and when they yawn open, whatever is inside comes out, and then they close again. But, they work better in privacy; they're shy, and this is true of humans and most animals. We seek privacy to allow our sphincters to do their jobs, jobs that at the most basic level have to do with hormone levels in the body. For example, oxytocin levels in blood rise when something big comes out (whether it's a baby or a bowel movement). Laughter is one thing that can help open the sphincters. I ask women to laugh when they're having a baby because it helps the process along; it also adds to oxytocin and endorphin levels. But on the converse, if someone is afraid or feels violated, for example, the sphincter can slam shut.

Gaskin has been known to illustrate this point in her birth classes. She puts a big silver bowl in the middle of the room, with a hundred-dollar bill in it. Anyone who can poop in the big silver bowl can have the hundred dollars. So far, no one's been able to.

So, here we are potty training, and the potty chair is pretty much in the middle of the room—even if only metaphorically speaking. The spotlight is on the potty chair, on the child and the poop. We're expecting the child to poop in the silver bowl, and it doesn't always work that way. The tricky part is that you can't give your child complete privacy when they are learning something. They can't be left alone because they most likely need your help in recognizing the feeling of needing to poop and manipulating the actual getting to and on the potty chair.

I generally find parents are not tolerant of any stalling on the child's part when it comes to poop. The parents have decided to potty train and expect everything to just flow the way it did in the relative privacy of the diaper. When things don't flow that smoothly, the parents confuse the delay with the child "not being ready." In fact, the complete opposite is true: the earlier you potty train, the less your child is aware of the general need for privacy during this bodily function. The older child will be very aware and will thus show increased resistance. As the cervix does, the anus relaxes in an environment that is gentle—an environment without a lot of fanfare and words. An environment that is relaxed, semiprivate, and perhaps filled with laughter. The more normal and routine you can make pooping for your child, the more relaxed the anus is going to be. The glaring spotlight of this whole process can back some kids up. That's totally normal. The analogy to labor carries through: when you are in labor, you want someone sure and steady by your side. You don't want someone overtalking with logic and reason. You don't want someone high-strung. And you certainly don't want anyone breathing down your neck to get it done.

Patience, consistency, and understanding are what will make this normal for your child. I realize that providing privacy is hard with a small child who is just learning a new skill, but there are some ways you can help. In the beginning stages of potty training,

I suggest you keep the potty chair wherever your child spends the most time, but that doesn't mean it has to be in the middle of the room. The pooping process can be discreet without being behind closed doors. You can be by your child's side but not all up in their business. (Seriously. Do not spread your kid's butt cheeks to check if the poop is coming. It's a hard urge to resist, but resist you must.) A really great trick is to get your child sitting for a poop and all of sudden think of something you need to do in the other room. Tell them to sit tight; you'll be right back. Nine times out of ten, the child will poop when you are gone for a minute. In fact, a huge telltale sign that it's time to potty train right now is when your child goes somewhere specifically to poop. Don't miss that window of opportunity!

The goal is to take that glaring spotlight off your kid and off this process. No one wants to poop with all eyes on them. Of course, a nice high five or fist bump once the deed is done is perfectly fine!

If your child isn't pooping in those first few days, relax. This isn't willful and it's not manipulation: it's totally normal, like a little performance anxiety.

Ina May Gaskin ends her discussion of sphincter muscles with this: "If someone is afraid or feels violated, the sphincter can slam shut." Of course, she's referring to the cervix and birth, and I'm referring to the anus and poop. Same difference. A sphincter by any other name is still a sphincter.

That brings us to the next logical point. Why on earth would a child feel afraid or violated during potty training? Well, for a lot of reasons, actually, none of which have to do with "readiness." I already mentioned the privacy issue: putting a glaring spotlight on a private function can feel violating. Of course, I'm not talking about the kinds of horrible violations that you sometimes see on the news—I'm talking about the embarrassing kind of violation, but nonetheless, on a primal level, it can feel violating. The same kind of embarrassing feeling of violation that makes us not want to blow a bunch of farts when we're in a public restroom and someone's in the next stall. I know you know what I'm talking about.

Let's look at why a child might be afraid of pooping on the potty. For starters, it's new. Toddlers are known routine lovers. Diapers have been their routine since about two hours after birth. Think about that. Your child may well have been in a diaper before they were even fed the first time! It's pretty crazy when you look at it.

I use many phrases to describe what a diaper might mean to a kid: a habit, a routine, an addiction, a security blanket. Behind the words is the same notion: pooping in a diaper is all your child has known. Now, you and I logically know about waste management, the toxicity of fecal matter, and the wonders of the sewer system, but once again, let's look at this through toddler eyes. Since the dawn of your kid's time, they have pooped in a diaper. Maybe they know you go elsewhere to do your business, maybe they know you don't wear a diaper, maybe they know other grown-ups go elsewhere to do their business. But probably not, because toddlers don't really give a crap about anyone but themselves. This is all totally normal and, I think, kind of cool. Anyway, all this is by way of saying not to expect your toddler to come to the logical conclusion that one day they too will be pooping in that same designated place. In fact, expecting anything logical at all from your toddler would be your first mistake. Sometimes I think we forget how new they are to the world and expect them to think logically.

Your kid, for probably around two years, has been pooping the only way they know how, and then one day, you ask them to poop elsewhere. Do you see how this could be met with resistance? Imagine if you came to visit me at my house and I told you that we only poop in the corner of my living room. I tell you up, down, and sideways that it's okay. We all do it. Really. I'll give you privacy. Please, please, poop in the corner of my living room. Don't worry! I'll clean it up! No matter what, it would still feel wrong because you know logically that it's unsanitary and you have long been conditioned to poop in the proper place.

Ahhh . . . the magic words: *conditioned to poop in the proper place.* How do you condition a small human, whose logical reasoning is not yet developed? Funny you should ask. I'll take consistency and repetition for $1,000. That is the name of the pooping game: consistency and repetition.

Why else might your child be afraid of pooping in the potty? If you are eating while reading this, you might want to stop for a bit.

All your child has known, in addition to a diaper, is the warm, cozy feeling of that poop against their butt. That feeling is normal. It feels safe, it's their routine. It seems pretty gross to us as grown-ups, but it feels really comfortable to kids, mostly because it's all they know. I've worked with kids who can say outright, "I like the warm feeling of my pee and poop in my diaper."

And of course, let's not forget the fear of the toilet itself. Over the years, I've heard of every manner of monsters that live in the toilet. It's all fun and games to flush until it's time to actually put their own tushies there. Again, looking through the kids' eyes, they don't understand where the toilet flushes to (dang logic). And then we ask them to expose a very personal, vulnerable part of their anatomy to this gaping chasm of God-knows-what. So, yeah, it can be scary. Some children will parlay that fear right over to the little potty, but most kids get a real kick out of seeing just what and how much they produced (which can be freakishly large) and dumping it in the toilet. This is why I always recommend a little potty chair; I think they are brilliant. The little pot keeps the poop at least semiclose. It's a literal way for them to see what came out of them. It can be scary to give up what feels like a big part of themselves and not have it close by, at least for a while. The little potty chair is tremendously useful in getting the right amount of squat to evacuate properly. If your child is having trouble pooping on the big toilet insert, try the little potty chair with books under their feet.

All in all, when you are potty training, you're redirecting a lifelong habit. It may be a short life thus far, but still, a lifelong habit. As with so many habits that are instilled for any length of time, it's best to stop the habit cold turkey. Have you tried to get a kid to stop sucking on a binky? What works is throwing the binky out and dealing with the fallout, if there is one. Do you think it would be effective to let the child have the binky for an hour in the morning but no other time? Probably not. Toddlers don't have the capacity to think like that. They don't know time. Same thing with diapers. Many parents take the fear or resistance as a sign that the child is not ready. This is not true. In fact, the longer you keep your child in diapers, the longer this habit gets entrenched, the more attached the child is to the habit, the more normal the warm feeling of pee and poop against their skin becomes. It becomes harder and harder with passing time to get the kid to give this up. The resistance and fear actually increase, which is what leads to epic power struggles.

Not Getting Any Poop at All

This problem has many different forms. The first couple of days, we can't really make a call because we are learning. We can't say for certain what's going on until we see a pattern emerge. *It's very common* for your child not to poop on the first or second day of potty training. There's a lot of pressure, even from the most chill parents, and there's some performance anxiety. This natural pressure is why we want to keep everything low-key and relaxed. Within this broad category of "no poops," there are a few variations.

If your child seems to be doing fine with peeing and attempting to sit to try to poop, don't worry at all about the poop. It will come. In this case, we want to be sure that your child doesn't get backed up and have a painful poop. I'd suggest an over-the-counter stool softener to help them out. You can also increase their fat. One mom I recently worked with gave her daughter a couple of teaspoons of coconut oil (she called it special honey), and her daughter pooped within hours.

If your child is clearly doing a poop dance—you know they have to go; they know they have to go; and they sit, pop up, sit, pop up, walk on tiptoes, and the like—it's okay. Don't try to rush them. I've seen this dance go on for up to ten hours. Reassure them that poop goes in the potty. Always use terms like "let go," "slide," "let it out," "drop"; in other words, think *passive* words. For kids, poop usually does tend to slide out and, in fact, they are doing much more work by holding it. Remind them that they can use either the little pot or the toilet insert. Some kids have a clear preference. Offer to read to them or just sit with them. Remember that this is a new sensation, and because it's new, it can be freaky. This dance and poop troubles never have anything to do with "readiness." Most often, the poop will come in due time, and it will land in the potty or toilet. The great news about popping on and off the potty is that they are trying to make it okay in their head. They're working it out both literally and figuratively.

What if the poop dance has gone on and on and on and, of course, the minute you aren't watching, it lands on the floor? For one or two poops, don't worry; it won't derail the process. Just remind your child that it's not okay to poop on the floor and that poop goes in the potty. Validate the feelings: "I know it feels very strange, and you must put your poop in the potty." If your child seems weirded out by pooping on the potty, you always want to validate that feeling. You are never, ever going to convince them that it doesn't feel strange or, at the very least, new.

If the poop comes the minute you turn your back—usually this poop is also done in the corner—this is great news. This child simply needs more privacy. As I've mentioned before, you can get them situated on the potty and then "forget" something in the other room. Nine times out of ten, the poop will come when you are out of the room. I've also worked with clients who put the potty chair where the child would previously go to hide to poop in a diaper: under the table, behind the couch, or even in a tent or fort structure.

I'll mention this again later, but often when a kid is doing an elaborate poop dance (walking around holding their butt, usually on tippy-toes, and it's very clear they have to go), the best approach is to back off. You can just say to them, "I can tell you have to poop. There's your potty, or you can use the big toilet." This is a perfect time to be sure you are not overtalking. You need to give them some room to make a good decision.

If you have done all of this and it seems like nothing is helping, be sure to go back to block 1. Pooping on the floor should come as a shock to your child like, *I can't believe that just happened.* And pooping in pants becomes a habit so fast it's ridiculous. For pooping in pants, you want to go back to block 1 and pantsless. This step down to block 1 will help you ascertain if the pants are what's tripping the child up. For pooping on the floor, try to figure out if your child has a general pooping time and watch them like a hawk during that time. I usually find that pooping on the floor really is a "dropped it like it's hot" deal in most cases.

If for some reason, usually because of needing to be in day care, your child continually poops in their pants, this is considered a version of withholding. Check out the Don't Panic section toward the end of this book.

At this stage, maybe you've gone three or even four days without a poop. And this is where things can start to go wonky with YOU. I emphasize *you* because you most likely will start freaking out. Maybe your kid pooped three times a day while diapered and going four days without a poop is making you nervous. Or maybe your little one is getting cranky or not eating a lot. This is when parents start going overboard, with begging, cajoling, bribing, or making huge promises. Every family I have ever worked with on pooping issues has made this mistake. Most parents have gone so far as to offer a trip to Disney for a single poop in the potty.

Here's the thing. I've already talked about rewards and why I don't love them. I think they're an okay tool to use briefly if you're confused as to whether you're dealing with an "I can't" or an "I won't." But in general, not pooping can't be fixed with a reward. It's usually constipation or withholding (a muscular reaction to anxiety). These are not within your child's control, no matter what it looks like.

I also know that panicking and trying all kinds of things all of the time smells like fear to the child and makes them more anxious. You need to be their calm, not contribute to their chaos. If the parents are scattered and anxious, that doesn't help calm a child.

It's good to come up with a few simple phrases that you can say repeatedly—something like, "I know this feels different. I'm right here if you need me. You can do it." Repeating something over and over is calming. Constantly switching tactics is not.

Standing to Poop

If your child wants to stand to poop or you know they were a standing pooper even in a diaper, you can catch the poop with the little insert cup that comes with the potty chair. The child usually sits within a few poops, so this is just a little bridge to sitting. It goes a long way in validating them and getting them on board with sitting.

Your Child Is Doing Great with Pee But Seems Afraid of Pooping

Now we'll discuss withholding. Withholding and constipation can go hand in hand: one can cause the other and vice versa. The best way to tell which one you're dealing with is whether your child seems to be a willing participant. If they are sitting when they have the urge to poop, and maybe grunting or bending forward, they clearly have to poop but can't, that's usually constipation. However, if they appear to be dancing around, maybe holding their butt and clearly have the urge but seem to be trying to stop it, this is most likely withholding. If they will not sit on the potty and instead request a diaper to poop in, this is withholding. Maybe they'll ask for a nap or bedtime in the middle of the day; this is code for wanting a diaper. It's withholding. Pooping in pants and not in the potty past the first week of potty training is also withholding.

Withholding often looks like a child is doing it on purpose. They are not. They are having a muscular reaction to anxiety, and it must be worked through. I have not found this being remedied by rediapering and assuming the child is "not ready"; in fact, they usually make it worse.

I can fix almost any problem with potty training. The hardest thing to fix is when you give your child a diaper to poop in upon request. This can go on long term and I've seen nightmares because of this. Please don't do this. I know it can feel like a minor thing, but it's not.

I don't know why this happens for some kids, but while it's not exactly common, it's not rare either. It seems to be the exact moment that the anus opens to release the poop that causes these kids to freak out; they go into fight, flight, or freeze. No amount of begging, bribing, rewards, or consequences will help. It's important to get help as soon as you can because this gets worse with time, but it is fixable. This usually requires one-on-one help; you can find my resources in the Don't Panic section.

If this is happening to your child, this is not your fault and has nothing to do with how old your child was when you started potty training. I have seen kids withhold while still in diapers. I have seen withholding in delayed potty training five-year-olds. Some kids withhold as babies, and for some, potty training seems to spark it. But you need to know that this is nothing you did or said. If you think you're dealing with constipation, an over-the-counter stool softener is your best bet.

Pooping Only in Nap or Night Diapers

I usually like to give this scenario a little time. For the first month of potty training, I tend not to worry about it as it often resolves on its own. However, if it continues for months OR it looks like your child is actively withholding until the diaper goes on, it needs to be addressed. This also goes for the child who poops the minute you put the diaper on and asks to be changed. In this case, night training is the answer. While it's a version of withholding, you won't know what you're truly dealing with until you take the diaper off and see what happens. A lot of kids are like, "Oh, I guess I'll just poop in the potty." But other kids show that they can withhold poop for a long time. If you are not ready to night train, that's fine. Then take it off your worry plate. Diapers are for one thing only, pee and poop. You can't keep one on your kid and expect them not to use it for what it's intended.

Constipation and Blockages

Most parents don't know this, but a child can be completely backed up AND still pooping several times a day. What happens is if their anus closes while mid-poop, it pinches a piece off, which can float back up, creating a backup. Often if the anus isn't opening fully, this happens. Usually this is marked by many smaller poops throughout the day or smears.

Blockages can also be present even though the child might be pooping regularly. We are not smooth inside. A dry piece of poop can get stuck in a nook somewhere in the GI tract. Every poop that slides by it sort of spackles more poop onto it. This blockage expands outward, not inward. Some kids can have a blockage as big as a small Nerf football. Yikes, right? This is marked most often by cluster pee accidents. The child will seem totally fine for a few days or even a couple of weeks, and then as the organs shift, the blockage starts banging into the bladder, creating many accidents in a row that take the child by surprise. In both cases, consult your pediatrician. Every pediatrician I've ever come across (and that's a lot) has recommended a clean-out with MiraLAX. You can call and check if that's appropriate for you.

Past Rectal Pain or Any Butt Trauma

Consider whether your child has had any sort of rectal pain in the past. I've worked with all kinds of kids who've had all kinds of butt trauma. Some kids have constipation from an early age. Some kids have needed surgery on their genitals or anus. Some kids have had blood in their stools. If your child has had any kind of rectal pain or butt trauma, naturally we want to make sure that pooping is effortless. I always suggest front-loading the process with a stool softener just to make sure that it's soft and easy to pass.

Once a kid has had some sort of butt trauma, they may anticipate it hurting during pooping and be a little freaked out. Whatever you do, don't repeat back the words *hurt* or *scared*. You can't encourage your child if you are repeating their words back to them. As long as you've used a stool softener, you can be sure it doesn't actually hurt, but we also don't want to invalidate your child's feelings.

We can acknowledge their fear without repeating those words by using phrases like, "I know this feels weird and new, and I know you can let your poop just slide right out. All you have to do is open your poop gate and the poop will come out." Words like *new*, *weird*, and *different* acknowledge the feeling. Saying that "poop will slide out" makes it feel easy as opposed to "push it out."

Your Child Is Really Trying to Make It to the Potty but Is One Second and a Half a Loaf Too Late

This kid is awesome, and we have to give them props for trying. They just need to recognize the feeling a little sooner. You can help them by showing them—drum roll, please—the Really Fun and Really Effective Play-Doh Poop Trick, a little trick that I find helps kids visually connect the feeling with what's happening. A lot of times they're not aware of what's happening with the musculature way down deep in their butt cracks. When they have this visual, it clicks: "Ooooh . . . so when this happens, I need to get to the potty." This is great for kids who seem to be doing their best to get to the potty but are not quite making it.

Get some Play-Doh—bonus points if you use brown. Make a fist. The spot where your thumb curls around your index finger is a reasonable facsimile of the anus. Ta-da! Now your visual is ready. Put the brown Play-Doh in your fist and squeeze some out. Yep: totally fun and maybe a little gross. Kids love it. Explain to them, "When your poop is here [tucked inside your fist] but wants to come out, you tell me. When your poop is here [squeezing out of the fist], it's already out, and it's too late." You can also explain what all happens with the anus opening.

This is usually fun and informative for the child. For most kids, a light bulb goes on for them. And for you, it's yet another parenting moment of thinking, *Never in my life would I have seen myself doing this.*

* * *

Phew. That's a lot of pooping information. Come back to this chapter later if you need to. Don't try to digest this all if it's your first time through the book. The biggest deal with poop is that you have to be calm regardless of what your child is doing. Remember that the opposite of "holding it" is letting go. Make it safe for your child to let go. That means you stay calm and steady.

CHAPTER 11

Prior Attempts at Potty Training

Over the years I've been called on increasingly to fix potty training attempts gone awry. Most people run into trouble because they've waited too long or have been too casual about it.

This chapter is for you if you've made any attempt at all to potty train that hasn't gone well. I want to be clear: I'm not saying this is your fault. But there are some classic mistakes if your potty training hasn't been successful.

Often with my clients, I'm not called in until the entire process has disintegrated into a huge disaster. Parents' nerves are frayed, if not completely shot. Kids are ridiculously resistant: pooping on floors, running and screaming from the potty chair, disrespecting and ignoring parents (who, to be fair, are pretty hysterical). I've seen it all. Potty training elicits all kinds of emotions from both your child and you. Still, sometimes what looks like chaos—once pulled apart—is relatively easy to fix. If you've attempted this and it's gone horribly wrong, I have a Don't Panic section toward the end of the book. Often I see what I call potty PTSD. If you are super anxious, you will have a hard time being a rock for your little one.

While every child and every situation is slightly different, I have divided troublesome trainings into four main categories:

1. Kind of potty trained
2. Mostly potty trained
3. Clueless
4. The child from hell

We'll go through each category and figure out what went wrong and how to fix it.

The Kind-of-Potty-Trained Child

This most often results from a "let's just put out the potty to get used to it" or a "we're just being really casual about this" attitude. Translation: you haven't really committed. Once you commit to potty training, your child's abilities will follow in short order.

Where to go from here? Just pick a day and begin. Follow all the instructions in chapter 5, "Ditch the Diapers! The How-To." This child is just waiting for you to show up with consistency. It doesn't much matter what the specifics are.

Maybe you haven't committed because they haven't shown much interest. To this, I say, they may *never* show that much interest. I think this is one of the main reasons parents put off potty training: some kids never, ever show interest. Many times a kid doesn't show interest, but that doesn't mean they're not capable. Don't make the mistake of waiting for your child. There's a great quote I keep hearing from parents again and again: "Wow. It's like he was just waiting for me to take off the diapers." Yes. Your child expects you to take the lead in life. It's good.

The kind-of-potty-trained child is an easy fix. With consistency and repetition, this child should be done in a short amount of time, as long as you just pick a day and start with block 1.

The Mostly-Potty-Trained Child

This kid is a little harder. If this seems to be your child, you probably potty trained without this book and maybe didn't have a clear plan. But now things seem frayed around the edges. They know what to do and when to do it, and they mostly do it just fine. But maybe it seems like they are holding pee or poop, or both, until they have a diaper on (at naps and bedtime). They may request a diaper to poop in. Or maybe it's frequent accidents. Once potty trained, there will be accidents occasionally but not on a regular basis. Whatever the case may be, you've gone a while but you still have potty training on your mind and everything looks a little messy.

I often compare this to the unraveling of a sweater. It starts with just a pull, but pretty soon, it unravels into a big mess. Or often it just feels messy around the edges. Or maybe you have the feeling that ever so slowly, your child is moving backward. For whatever reason and however it happens, you just don't feel that you're over the finish line. In almost all cases, this is because you're still using diapers for night and nap. For this child, it's absolutely best to just give up all diapers. You can go back and breeze through the blocks of learning. It can be super helpful to see if they are successful with the potty while naked and the trouble comes when you try to put clothes on. I urge you to review chapter 10, "Poop." Sometimes frequent accidents are due to constipation or withholding.

Getting rid of all diapers and night and nap training seems to clear this situation. I've also found it helpful to run through the blocks again very quickly, whether you used this book originally or not. A lot of parents resist this because the child seems mostly done. But seeing where the glitch might be is very useful. Whenever I work privately with a client and this is the scenario, I have them go back to block 1. We need to see how the child does with no obstacles (pants being an obstacle). Sometimes there's an obvious place where the learning got stuck.

Running through the blocks and night and nap training is the best way to handle this situation. And if you hear "mostly potty trained" and automatically think "mostly dead" from *Princess Bride,* you are my people.

The Clueless Child

This child shows no indication of knowing what the hell you are talking about when you say "potty." Assuming there are no emotional or developmental delays, the truly clueless child is probably too young for potty training (which isn't to say it can't be done, just that it will take longer). Remember that the truly clueless child will pee as they're walking, slip on the pee, and still not know what just happened. Unless you are potty training well under twenty months or your little one has significant delays, there is little chance that your child is actually clueless.

The younger the child, the longer the learning curve will be, which is not at all to discourage you! Older kids have behavioral stuff that younger kids don't, so that's a huge bonus.

If you feel that your child is absolutely clueless, it's okay to reset and start over in a couple of months.

Often, however, parents think they are dealing with cluelessness but it's really a glitch in learning or some behavioral stuff that we'll discuss in a couple of later chapters. For instance, a twenty-eight-month-old child who is just "not getting it" isn't clueless. Usually something else is going on.

The Child from Hell

In my work, I see all kinds of reactions to potty training. The child from hell comes in a couple of forms. Sometimes it looks like extreme resistance. Sometimes they just don't seem to care and nothing you do can make them care. Sometimes they seem truly scared and sometimes they're flat-out hysterical. And sometimes it looks like an "eff you; I'm not doing this, and you can't make me."

Often I see this in a third or fourth child, and these kids tend to be a little feral; they tend to be what I call your "freedom child." I say this in the best of ways. They ignore the rules and do what they want because they know you're tired and busy. They're fun and probably your favorite because they go with the flow and do for themselves. They trail the big kids and know way more than they should. They also have older kids who do a lot for them, and they tend to be mischievous. Of course, this can be any kid, but I typically find it's not your first child. I love these kids, but they don't give AF, and that shows up in potty training.

Of course, the child from hell can certainly be anywhere in the birth order and of any age, though most are well over three years old. Typically you've made a couple of attempts at potty training and had to throw in the towel due to their high reaction (or the aforementioned, you're busy and tired). You've been told by everyone around you to just "wait till they're ready" and you're exhausted or nearly worried to death, so you do just that. But your child is getting older and a deadline may be approaching (usually needing to be fully trained for preschool or camp).

The important thing to remember is that in most cases I see where the parents describe a child from hell, it's not the child actively trying to push your buttons. That can certainly happen, but most often it's because of a true anxiety, poop or pee withholding, or you, the parents, are (unknowingly) putting too much pressure or you didn't have a clear plan and things got really scattered.

It's all okay! You CAN potty train even the most difficult kids and you CAN potty train at any age. You just need to be aware of what's really behind the struggle. If you didn't use this book with your prior attempts, I encourage you to read it from the beginning to the end and determine what and where things went south. For example, many parents attempt to potty train right from a diaper to underwear. They end up seeing nothing but accidents. Or maybe you got locked into power struggles due to overprompting and asking too often. When you have a clear idea of what went wrong, it's a relatively easy fix.

The child who doesn't care is a little trickier. Sometimes we have to help build the idea of pride in self-mastering this skill. I maintain that every child has an "in": your child almost always has something they care about. We then can work with the grain of their personality and use that as leverage.

Trickier still is the child with a lot of anxiety. Often this presents as "scared of the potty." Sometimes it's right out of the gate, and other times you may actually have a good start for a few days and this anxiety comes out of the blue. And the trickiest of all is the child who seems to be directly telling you to eff off by peeing or pooping wherever they want. Some kids really do seem to come out of the womb with boxing gloves on and will fight you on everything. You are probably very aware of it if this is your child, and in fact this is a good way to distinguish what you are actually dealing with.

Sometimes parents have a hard time differentiating between anxiety and these contentious kids. Pee and poop withholding can often look like the child is doing it on purpose (they are not), and things can escalate so much that it looks like it's all behavior. In my experience, if your child has been what parents describe as "an angel child" and you're seeing crazy resistance, this is usually anxiety. On the flip side, if you know you have that kid with boxing gloves on, you're most likely going to have that same kid for potty training.

And here's the final kicker. If you've had a couple of potty training attempts and they've been an unmitigated disaster, you probably have what I call potty PTSD. You are now nervous or anxious yourself and will have a hard time being an effective teacher. My sincerest hope is that this book gives you a solid plan and helps you feel more confident about this whole process.

These issues don't indicate "not ready," and you should work through them as soon as you're able. I don't typically see these resolve with more time; in fact, I see them get further ingrained.

CHAPTER 12

Day Care Struggles

Day cares can throw a major wrench in the potty training process. I used to believe that everything hinged on having your day care on board. But I've changed my mind a bit and have helped many parents negotiate success with or without the day care's cooperation.

Before you even *begin* potty training, find out your day care's policy. Most larger day cares have a formal policy. Home day cares and nanny situations may not have a formal policy, but they'll still have their own opinion of how this should go. So *find out*. Ask many questions. Many day cares say they will work with you, but you'll find later that they really won't. Alternately, they may have some weird notions of what they can and can't do. It's best to find out what they do before you walk in on a Monday morning after a weekend of potty training and are shocked. Some day cares are well versed in potty training and help as much as they can. The bummer is that most aren't, so here's the un-sugarcoated version of what's going on.

In September 2012, I was inundated with emails from all over the country. These were official positions from day cares specifically stating that children MUST be fully potty trained while wearing a pull-up. The diaper was not to be removed until the child could stay dry in said pull-ups for two solid weeks. I have no idea what went on in the world to create this official stance. But it was very strange coming from so many different places in the country simultaneously.

Somehow this became the "official" policy of many day cares. I get it. It's not easy for a day care to deal with potty training. Not having to deal with it is a huge load off their minds and hands. Potty training a large group of children isn't easy, I realize. I also realize that each state may have its own regulations regarding certain aspects of potty training (such as cleanup and having a child go unassisted to the bathroom). Still, I want to point out the ludicrousness of this supposed policy.

How on earth can you expect a child to learn a new behavior while actively engaging in the old behavior? Have you ever tried to get a kid to eat broccoli while they're munching on candy? Or let's say you want to cut down on TV watching. By this logic, you should keep the TV on until the child is ready to watch less. *This is nearly impossible* and actually requires a huge amount of skill and thought from a *child*. It really makes my head almost explode.

The people who should be the most informed about child development are all just nodding their heads as if this new recommendation makes perfect sense. WTF?

So, back to day cares. What I've heard from many providers is they simply don't have the time to attend to a child with the speed necessary during potty training. In other words, they know that when a kid's gotta go, they've gotta go *now*, and they can't respond that quickly.

What is more important than learning a life skill? Imagine if a day care offered to potty train. Holy crap: they'd have a waiting list five years long and could charge double. What are they doing that's more important than that? Learning shapes and colors and dramatic play is all well and good, but learning to put pee and poop in the potty? Even better.

The biggest problem with not having a supportive day care is that you are essentially getting screwed, especially if you are a single parent or both parents work full time. (Though I'm sure you're used to getting screwed by everything at this point. Right?) Because immediately after day care comes preschool, and preschools demand absolute, full-on potty trained.

Ridiculous, yes? Yes. It ticks me off to no end. But the reality is that I'm sure your day care does care wonderfully for your child, and I'm sure you don't have much of a choice, so we'll deal with what we've got. I'll go through the best way to set you and your child up for success and how to deal with the less ideal scenarios.

Take off as many days in a row as possible to start potty training. Something like a three-day weekend with one extra day tacked on is usually great. I know this is not the ideal way to spend a precious vacation day, but it's worth it in the end. If you can take more time off, that's even better. I've already made my case for the most days possible at home. If day care is more a social thing and not a necessity, consider keeping your child home for a couple of extra days.

In that time frame, while potty training, *really* try to learn your child's pee pattern. That's how much and how often your child typically pees after x amount of fluid. The good news is that most day cares have a sort of formal routine for snacks and such, so usually fluid intake is controlled. Still, you want to have an overall awareness so you can pass on information. As you are potty training, be sure you are saying to your child what you would like *them* to say. Remember when you were teaching "bye-bye," you probably very naturally said *their* words: "Bye-bye, Grandma!" Right? Probably in a high squeaky voice too. And eventually they started saying "bye-bye."

Same thing with potty training. So as you are getting them to the potty you would say, "Mama, go potty" or "Mama, pee." Something along those lines. This is something that *all* parents should do, but it's especially important for you because, ideally, we need your child asking to pee as soon as possible when they return to the day care (realistically, though, self-initiation doesn't fully begin until three to six weeks after your start date).

Don't worry about the nap diaper at day care. Send a diaper. It's a pretty useless fight that you probably won't win. I think it's probably easiest for all involved to not do night and nap training at the beginning. It's especially hard for single or two out-of-home working parents.

The commando issue is a big one that day cares resist. I think a lot of people are weirded out by the idea of no underwear. I also think it's with good cause for poop accidents. If your child is a good pooper with regard to potty training and self-initiates poop (many kids do before they even get the peeing down pat), some parents choose not to say anything, send their child commando, and beg forgiveness instead of asking permission. The big problem is that wearing underwear can be too confusing for your child in the beginning. The snugness creates a muscle memory of a diaper, and the covering suggests privacy. I can almost bet you that your child will have more accidents if you put undies on them too soon. So you may have to rush the undies into the training if you have very limited time.

The biggest issue of all is that we have no control over what happens at day care, and we will never know exactly how it goes down. We want to keep directions to the teachers brief and direct and not overwhelm them, so we'll run through some basic solutions.

Let's say it's gone pretty well at home. Your child is getting it but isn't done by any means. The day you return to day care, fill the teacher in. When you get there, take your child to the bathroom and show them the ropes and anything particular to school. If the bathroom is not accessible to your child, ask to have a potty chair in the room. If they don't allow that, I'd seriously consider moving day cares, if that's an option. It's *imperative* that your child have access to the bathroom.

If you are potty training during the summer or between switching from day care to preschool, see if the teacher can send you pictures of the bathroom setup. This will go a long way in helping to prepare your little one.

I occasionally run into day care in a setting where the bathroom is down the hall and under lock and key. There's no way your child is far enough along in the process to hold it that long. Again, I know you may have no control or choice when it comes to day care. In that case, I'd hold off potty training or know that you'll probably have a long learning curve ahead of you.

Tell your child clearly who is available to help them. This is even ideal to start using these names while at home. Name names, point, and have a discussion with the adult and your child. Day care can get confusing, and you want your child to be sure they know who to ask for help, even if it seems totally obvious. In pointing out a source of help, scope out their favorite teacher. There's always a preferred staff at day care. Look for the good cop—the sweet one, the patient one. Find her (or him) and give directives to that one. Don't go to the meanie if there is one. It's perfectly fine if they take the children to the bathroom at set intervals.

It's not how I potty train at home, but with groups of children, it works wonders. The herd mentality works in our favor here. They need to be taking the children at least once an hour, preferably every forty-five minutes or so. I had a day care tell me they didn't have the time except for once every two hours!!! That's too long (and kinda bullshit if you ask me). On the flip side, I've had another day care take a child every fifteen minutes, and that's too often.

If you know your child's pee-pee dance, let the care provider(s) know. Again, there are obvious classic dances, like hopping from foot to foot, but some kids get really quiet, and some may get louder. Whatever your kid does, let the day care know about it if you can.

Arrange a special signal between the teacher and your child. The best one is having your child tug on the teacher's arm. I don't know why, but children sometimes get embarrassed about asking to go to the potty and drawing attention to themselves. You'd think pooping in your pants at the sand table would be at least equally embarrassing, but it's not. Go figure. Anyway, a nonverbal signal can nip this in the bud.

Ask the teacher to please save your child's spot whenever they go to the bathroom. This is a big one. Many children are fearful of losing their spot or the toy they were playing with. Once they know they won't lose these, they are more likely to take potty breaks.

Make sure the teacher isn't staring them down while they try to use the potty. Every place has a different arrangement. If there's a stall with low toilets, the teacher can take your child to the bathroom and semiclose the door. If there are potty chairs in the room, great; just discourage hovering. I worked with a little girl, Emily, who was doing fine at home. However, at day care, she would hold it and hold it and she would try to sit but wouldn't pee. The teacher was getting aggravated. After some questioning, it turns out she was hovering over Emily, pretty much demanding that something happen. It won't work that way. Once the teacher started being more casual and averting her own eyes, Emily did great. The same deal applies for pooping. Pooping needs privacy.

Check out where the other kids are in the potty training process. If your child is the first one diving in, use that. Tell your child they're the first and they can show them all how to do it. I'll be honest, though; it's hard when your child is the first or the only. It's a pretty raw deal to have to pay attention to your bodily fluids when no one else is. If your child is the last to be trained, use it. Tell them who else is doing this so they are not alone. Having a bathroom buddy can make this whole thing much easier.

If day cares use a reward system, it's fine. Just stay steady at home with no rewards. If your child asks for one at home, simply say, "Oh, no. That only happens at school, honey." In my experience, it's never been a problem or confusing. It's not ideal, but the school has to deal with that potential treat monster. The children I've worked with have never had an issue with things being different at home.

Those are all the big things. You don't want to overwhelm your day care with a huge list of instructions. You should get a sense of how they are going to be with this by asking a few simple questions. A sample conversation might go something like this:

Hi! We're going to start potty training Sally over the long weekend. We believe the best approach is to remove daytime diapers. We'd be delighted if you could help us in this process. How do you typically handle potty training? I'm sure you have vast experience. We'd like to combine forces with you for the most successful outcome for Sally.

Do you take the children who are potty training to the washroom at certain intervals? How often? How many accidents do you allow before requesting a diaper be put on?

As long as Sally is showing progress I'm sure we can work on this together.

I really value you as Sally's care provider. We feel the timing is right for potty training. Anything we can do to assist you, please let us know.

In saying this, you've stated what you would like in no uncertain terms, you've done a fair amount of transparent ass kissing, and you've stated how much you value the day care, all good things. You most likely will get a response like, "We'll work with you, however you're doing it." Sounds great, but ask those questions! I've had too many parents gloss over this and end up with a nightmare.

I've found that day cares can cop an attitude regarding who knows more about child development. They may say, "It won't happen till age three," or "Children can only potty train in pull-ups." Somehow it becomes a little power struggle about who knows more. The best way is simply to state your desires for your child. A good day care will do their best to work with you.

You really want to get a sense of your care provider's attitude. You'll be able to tell by body language, tone, and the words they choose how they are going to act. Again, this is where some day cares get huffy about their authority.

Don't fight. Instead, gently prod and fully express how you'd like potty training handled. Some day cares have a written policy that states your child must stay in diapers until potty trained. Gently try to work your way around this. The best way is to act *totally* stupid, like, "Gee. That's weird. I would think it'd be hard to learn something new while actively taking part in the old. Hmmm. That seems very odd."

If it's looking like they won't budge, that's okay too. As I stated at the beginning of this chapter, I used to think this was the end of the world, but it's not. I used to write letters on behalf of my clients, even talk to day cares on the phone. Moms would be getting ulcers trying to knock sense into them. And, yes, *we got our way.* But then we had day care providers on edge—they were nervous wrecks, totally overprompting and hovering. Not good. We need this process to be stress free for your child. An anxious provider is going to derail things even more than a diaper will.

If your child *has* to wear a diaper at day care, there's just not much you can do about it. What you *can* do is keep with the (diaper-free) system at home. Most parents figure out a way to make this work. It should look something like this. When you drop them off at day care, go to the bathroom together for a pee and put the diaper on them while in the bathroom. Tell them, "This is in case there's an accident. You should tug on Miss Suzy's arm when you have to go pee, or you can come by yourself" (if that's true). Say no more and no less. You're not letting them off the hook of potty training, and you're not suggesting they just use the diaper to pee in. You are being vague on purpose. You are assuming they will use the diaper as underpants. It's a hard way to potty train, but it's doable.

Same deal for pickup. Go to the bathroom for a last pee before the trip home. Take off the diaper and leave it there (in the proper receptacle, of course). Say, "We're going home now, and you don't use diapers at home. Remember to tell me when you are going to go pee."

What this does is reinforce the notion that diapers are equated with day care. It's a day care thing, and, oddly, this generally makes sense to the child. What happens in Vegas stays in Vegas, right? If the day care is okay with changing diapers, so be it.

Having to do diapers at day care is not preferable, and it can make potty training drag out a bit but not indefinitely. Still, having a stress-free environment (rather than fighting with day care) will make this much easier for all of you. And be sure to be honest and bring lots of clothes.

If your child is having very little success at home—and I mean *very* little—it's okay. Some kids do take longer to potty train than others. In such a situation, be sure to check in with the day care. Tell them you'd love to give it a shot at day care without a diaper to see if they are just being obnoxious at home.

I know this is shocking, but our kids can be angels with other people and save all their crappy behavior for us, the parents. Enlist the day care's help as a resource: "I know he's so good for you. We've done potty training this weekend and it's going . . . eh. Would you be willing to try today to see if he does well with you?" This usually gets a favorable response, again thanks to some transparent ass kissing. And many times this works. Most kids do well at day care, particularly if they go to the bathroom in groups at timed intervals.

So, in summary, find out the day care policy and how they handle potty training, in detail. If they are willing and able, go for it. If they seem resistant, try to bring them to the light. If they insist on the diaper at day care, proceed with potty training when your child is at home.

The thing is, we can't hold off potty training until day care gets on board. The older your child gets, the harder potty training becomes. You also will not have much time to wrap things up before preschool starts. My business gets very intense around August, when suddenly there's a mad dash to potty train for preschool. That can put too much pressure on the process and totally implode. You want to gently push the issue as much as possible, but it's doable to potty train while your child is in full- or part-time day care, even a resistant one.

The bottom line is not to be crazy with day cares. They do provide care for your child for a substantial part of the day. They are only human and can deal with only so much. We don't want them to start having a bad attitude toward your child. The best thing is to really do that data collection in the first few days; looking for their pee dance and their pee patterns so you can pass that on to the day care or other caregivers.

CHAPTER 13

Behavior versus Potty Training

This is probably the trickiest issue I address in this book: separating out behavior from potty training. There is a lot for your child to learn when potty training. Certainly the first few days, and maybe even the first few weeks, are full of learning. Learning by nature requires making some mistakes and having some accidents. However, there is a difference between learning and behavior. A few different behavioral things will probably come up. One, of course, is what we might categorize as "bad" behavior. I put that word in quotes because all behavior is a communication and it would be wonderful if we didn't think of it as "bad." Included under this umbrella is classic limit testing, game playing, not listening, and bedtime struggles. Then we have another category of weird behaviors that crop up around potty training.

I first need to cover some ground about boundaries and limits, and then will look at specific behaviors I've seen in potty training. Boundaries and limits have a bad rap in parenting of late. They can seem mean or draconian or too authoritarian. Many parents don't believe in any sort of consequence or discipline. Let me state outright: I do not recommend or believe in hitting a child. Ever. However, discipline (the Latin root word from *disciple*, to teach) is needed as in teaching is needed. Your child needs to know what's acceptable and what's not.

Chances are you are potty training somewhere around the two-year-old mark, and around the same time, you may see some other two-year-old behavior. This may well be the very first time you are seeing your child act up, but it's normal. The terrible twos (and even more trying, the threenager) aren't just a cliché; they are real. In the course of normal development, your child must test limits. It's their job. They need to find out where the fence is, so to speak. The reason you physically fence in your yard is so your child can't wander and get lost. Limits and boundaries are the fence in your child's psyche. With them intact, just as in your yard, your child feels safe and secure knowing where they can and can't go.

A trend in modern parenting is to assume that the child is capable of deciding good things for themselves without being provided any boundaries or limits. This is not the case. I often look to the Montessori system for examples of how to allow children to make decisions while also providing boundaries. Within a certain framework, the children are free to make choices, but they are not free to do whatever it is they want. The children all eat lunch together. They typically are in charge of certain aspects; setting the table, pouring the drinks, laying out food. However, they don't have full access to the snack fridge and it is not left up to them to decide when they are hungry; you would have mayhem. The children all go outside together, whether one is tired or not. Our children require some fences. Within those fences, we can allow for tremendous freedom.

Bringing Up Bébé by Pamela Druckerman was released to a torrent of mixed press. Druckerman claims that the French in general are doing a better job of parenting than Americans are, largely because of the French notion of *cadre*, loosely translated as "framework." French children are given a strict framework, but within that they have tremendous freedom. There is much I don't like in the book—or rather there's much about what the French supposedly do and don't do that I dislike—but I agree fully with *cadre*.

What I see in both my life and my work is that a lot of parents struggle with providing freedom within boundaries. In our quest to raise free-thinking, independent children, we are not providing enough of a framework for them to feel safe. I mentioned *Simplicity Parenting* by Kim John Payne at the beginning of this book. I can't recommend this book highly enough: Payne is brilliant and eloquent on this topic. He says that raising children is like building a pyramid. The widest part at the bottom is the foundation. That is made up of "governing," and takes place roughly from birth to age six. Next is the middle of the pyramid, made up of a "gardening" phase that takes place from roughly six to twelve years old. And at the top is the "guiding" phase, which is the way he recommends parenting children ages twelve to eighteen. He suggests that most parents have flipped the pyramid and are trying to guide children when what they need is governing—that is, providing boundaries and limits (and not cruel or harsh punishment). When a parent tries to guide a child whose prefrontal cortex—the area of the brain responsible for logic, reason, executive functioning—isn't fully formed, it backfires. Then that parent is left to govern when the child is older and should only need guiding. I see this in my own community. I see children raised with no limits or boundaries who are wild and at times out of control by the time they are five or six.

Payne also uses the analogy of you, the parent, driving a car. Imagine the anxiety your child would feel if you were driving, they were in the back seat, and you had no idea where you were going. I've extrapolated that idea even further. Imagine if your child were *responsible for giving you the directions* and that you just followed those directions. Go left. Go straight. No. Left. Wow. You'd soon be lost. That's where things can get mucky with the oft-touted child-led model of parenting. You can child lead in that you listen to and validate them, but you simply cannot follow your child's lead through life. You will both get lost. The car you are driving is life, and it's your job to know where you are going. Ironically, many of the parents I've worked with and have known in my personal life are striving to give their child a "free" childhood. Still, how free is your child if he is fully responsible for the direction the car is traveling in? It's very anxiety provoking. A truly free childhood should be about chocolate or vanilla, and little else.

All this is particularly true if you have a spirited or strong-willed child. I often work with parents who have a child fitting this description. This child is usually challenging in general and will be challenging when it comes to potty training as well. Still, this child needs boundaries and limits just as much as, if not more than, your garden-variety kid.

Sometimes behavior kicks up during potty training, and because potty training is so fraught with emotion, it becomes hard to pull it apart from behavior. I also find that parents will put up with all kinds of behavior during potty training that they wouldn't in other circumstances. For example, one of the biggest challenges parents today face during potty training is getting their child to sit on the potty. Yes, you can read to them or sing to them. But really, when you ask your child to sit to go potty, your child should sit. Now, to a lot of people, that sounds harsh, but if you take it out of the context of potty training, it sounds perfectly reasonable. Say it's time to sit down for dinner, and your child keeps bouncing up (assuming they aren't buckled to a chair of sorts). You tell your child to sit and they don't. How do you handle that? I'm asking because whatever your response is, that's how you're going to handle it during potty training. When it's dinnertime, it's time to sit and eat. When it's potty time, it's time to sit on the potty. Same thing.

Whenever you encounter behavior during potty training, do your best to put it in a different context. That will help you figure out how best to respond in the context of potty training. It's totally your parenting call. For some reason, potty training seems to scare us, the parents, and that can skew our normal boundaries.

Many parents say, "I don't feel comfortable making him sit." I agree. I don't think you should force your child to sit. However, it's worth pondering just how fearful we've become of transition to the potty. Many parents fear doing *anything* negative around potty training. Using a firm or stern voice sounds negative to these parents, and they're concerned about a negative association with it. But here's the rub: your child may need a slightly negative association to learn that a behavior is unacceptable.

Let's go back to being neutral about everything. If you don't flavor that with some sort of "good" or "bad," your child will just learn that everything's okay. For some parents, that's cool. Maybe they live out in the woods and are raising a slightly feral kid. Hey!

I'm all for it. You can raise your child however you want. My gripe is when we then flip it on them, when there comes a time that they must listen to you or they must have good behavior, like going to school and sitting still. Then it's not fair to the child that we've made everything okay and suddenly it's not. As a veteran home-schooler, I've seen all kinds of families, and I love the feral ones, but that's not for everyone, and so if it's not the trajectory of your life, you must set boundaries right from the start.

Regardless of your parenting style, I would argue that there are nonnegotiable times in which we set firm boundaries because we must. I bet every single one of us has held our child down and strapped them into the car seat, even when they are kicking, screaming, and hitting. We do it because we must go somewhere, and we need them to be safe. Has your child ever been traumatized by that and never wanted to sit in the car seat again? I'm guessing no. Again, I'm not saying you should force your child onto the potty or strap them down or anything remotely like that. I'm just pointing out that this fear of traumatizing a child by conveying the message that you mean business has gotten a little bit out of control. Another thing to keep in mind is the difference between the child you have and the child you want. You have the kid you have, not necessarily the kid you want. This is especially true when potty training.

I can give you suggestions about any special circumstances you may have, but we cannot change your zebra's stripes. Still, this is hard for us to admit and hard to remember. We all want a well-behaved, loving, courteous child. We got what we got. Still, our love is fierce. While you are potty training, be careful not to linger in the land of "I wish they'd just..." We can deal with what we have, but we cannot deal with a fantasy. Your kid comes with all their own crazy, their own stuff, their own DNA. There's another aspect to the kid you have. If your child has a particular "problem"—say they're whiny, resistant, or prone to histrionics and tantrums— you are going to have this same kid when you are potty training. Still, I see parents who somehow think potty training is going to happen in a bubble—that all the other behavior the child exhibits is somehow not going to appear while potty training. This is a big transition, so these behaviors will not only be there—they might even get magnified for a short period of time.

Again, it's all good. Just keep your expectations level and your love big.

Whatever your child's personality is, I can't change that or fix it; that's built in. If your child is exhibiting behavior you don't like or you feel is disrespectful, you will most likely see that very same behavior while potty training. What I *can* tell you is how to deal with some of the behaviors you find in potty training.

If you're not sure whether you're dealing with behavior, look inside, and see how you're feeling. If you are feeling sad or a little heartbroken that this isn't going as you intended, chances are your child needs more learning. If you feel that you are being played, if you feel angry, or if you feel like strangling your kid, I'll bet it's behavior. Most times, parents have a good sense when they are dealing with behavior but don't do anything because they are terrified of "traumatizing" the child. Having boundaries and following through is not going to traumatize your child in any sense. The key thing with boundaries is that you have to be sure you're clear about them, that you communicate them often to your child, and you follow through. Just recognize that potty training can coincide with your child discovering their autonomy and their own power and they may start to use that.

A common example of this is limit testing. This usually shows up as a kid who has shown they can pee and poop in the toilet, and then somewhere along the way, be it two days or two weeks, they may start peeing elsewhere. It may look as if they don't care. It may be that they laugh and say, "Look! I peed on the couch." It comes in many different styles and flavors but it most certainly looks like this is on purpose. It might feel like they're totally dicking you around. This is classic limit testing, which often gets a bad rap. Limit testing is literally your kid testing your limit—not your breakdown limit, mind you, but your line in the sand. Without any emotion, this can be translated as "What are you going to do about it?"

I think it's nearly impossible to hear that phrase without attitude but try. What ARE you going to do about it? They're testing the waters to see if you are indeed going to do something about it. And if you're not, then they can carry on with it.

Again, I don't feel comfortable telling specifics here, but we can go back to that notion of putting this in another context. If you are certain that this is behavior and not just a mistake, I'd handle this as if your child looked right at you as they poured a drink out onto the rug. Think of what you would do in addressing these accidents-on-purpose. But that being said, check in with yourself. Had you not prompted them in a while? Did you have the thought to do so and it slipped your mind? Was there some support you could have given that would've helped your child? Also, bear in mind that many accidents happen during screen time and many parents think this is behavior because they didn't want to pause to

BEHAVIOR VERSUS POTTY TRAINING

pee. While this is true, remember that children this age cannot distinguish between the screen and real life. They get sucked in and are bound to have accidents. You must hold off screen time until you get a good pee.

In general, if you sense a pattern of behavior linked to a certain activity (screens, playgrounds), do not engage in a power struggle. Remember the trick of holding off the activity until they pee, which isn't a bribe: "Sure, you can watch your show when you've peed. Let me know when you're done." "Yup, we sure can go to the park. Let me know when you're done peeing and then we can go."

Rewards and/or Consequences

I don't really love rewards while potty training. I know it's common, but I see full-blown disasters. Some people swear by sticker charts, but if that has worked, it's because they're lucky. Kids may enjoy getting a sticker, but it's a very rare two- or three-year-old who has the capability of understanding that an x amount of stickers for staying dry will yield a bigger prize.

Consequences are okay if you're certain you're dealing with behavior. Often, natural consequences are best; if your child pees their pants at the park, you leave because they're wet. That's a great one. Rewards can be a useful tool if you're uncertain whether you're dealing with behavior or a glitch in learning. If a kid can do it for an M&M, they can do it without it too. I find it often helps parents have a clearer sense of what's going on and can then act accordingly.

If you think you're going to use rewards or consequences, they must be small and immediate. Behavior in the morning with a consequence of no playdate tomorrow won't cut it. You can't use something hours away as a consequence. Your child won't track that. A reward should also be small and immediate, making it what I call "an emotionally clean transaction": you did this, and I gave you that.

For consequences, it's absolutely key that you set up the parameters beforehand with your child. This is what will allow them room to make a good choice: "If you pee your pants at the park, we'll have to leave." If you don't do this, the consequence will seem punitive, and therefore is a punishment, which is not effective in learning.

Of note, do not reward for "staying dry." That's a lofty concept that requires two steps in the thinking process and requires executive functioning, which is not their strong point at this age. Simply give them the thing immediately after they pee and be VERY careful not to slip into bribery. Again, use this as a tool, and ditch it as soon as possible.

A Couple of Weird Behaviors

Peeing only outside is an odd one that I'm suddenly hearing a lot about. My short answer is going to sound curt, but it's really all I've got: don't let them. Listen, I love peeing outside, and I think every family should have a designated pee bush that everyone can use while playing in the yard. But generally just going outside is a pitfall of summer potty training. It's okay in a pinch, but if it looks like it's headed to becoming a habit, you should nip it in the bud.

If it has already become a habit, it's time to go back inside for a few days until your little one gets it all in the potty.

Another of these behaviors is excessive sitting on the potty. I've had only a few cases of this but it can be concerning. The child somehow gets overly concerned about accidents and decides to sit on the potty all day. I recently heard from a family that their child would even fall asleep on the potty. Kids, especially toddlers, go sideways about the weirdest things. In cases like this, I think it's wise to pass along the potty to "the next kid who needs it" and just use the big toilet or at least remove the potty during the night and into morning. Be careful not to make a big deal about accidents or harp on them. With one little girl, this seemed to be the manifestation of a larger anxiety issue, and she was able to get past it with a few sessions with a therapist.

I'm sure there are many other weird behaviors out there. I think the biggest thing to remember is to separate out parenting from potty training. The easiest way to do this is to put it in another context. For example, with the peeing outside. If your child would only eat outside, you would be clear that it's not acceptable: "You come and sit at the dinner table." You would probably lock the door so they can't get out. For some reason, when any sort of behavior creeps into potty training, parents get wiggly about being firm and having boundaries. I get it! It feels like a delicate process, and you don't want to rock the boat once you see an iota of progress. But in the majority of cases, all that's needed is firm or stern boundaries and following through with them.

CHAPTER 14

Younger Than Twenty Months, Older Than Thirty-Six Months

I always recommend starting potty training between twenty and thirty months with a slightly pushed-out window to thirty-six months. In my vast experience, that's usually the easiest time. Of course, it is totally possible to potty train both before twenty months and after thirty months.

I have no vested interest in when you potty train. My job is to let you know potential hot spots at whatever age you do this. I've had people contact me on the verge of a breakdown because they are just picking up this book and their child is past my recommended age range. It's okay! Certain ages make things easier, but that doesn't mean it's impossible. So let's dive into what to expect if you are potty training either earlier or later than my recommended time frame.

Younger Than Twenty Months

It is completely possible to potty train under twenty months. I've worked with many clients who potty train between sixteen and twenty months. But if your child is in any sort of day care situation, this may be next to impossible if you don't have their full support. And by that I mean they are actively helping with potty training. I have worked with a few day cares that support this age for potty training, but the majority of day cares will fight tooth and nail that this is too young. Interesting side note: Maria Montessori believed that potty training should happen between twelve and eighteen months and knew this was a process, not a three-day-and-done deal. Here are a few things to consider if you're potty training in this age range.

LACK OF LANGUAGE

A lot of parents want to potty train at this age but are concerned because the child doesn't have a lot of language yet. I've discussed this elsewhere, but it's worth mentioning again. Think about this: your child is constantly communicating with you and is most likely at the point-and-scream stage. While this is a delightful way to communicate, it's not always effective when potty training. The easiest thing is to teach your child a sign for pee, poop, or just going to the bathroom. This can be official sign language or you can just make something up. Anecdotally, I consistently hear reports of boosts in language during the potty training process.

PULLING DOWN THE PANTS AND PHYSICALLY MANIPULATING CLOTHES

I discussed this in chapter 4, "Mental Preparation," if you missed it. You definitely want to start working on your child being able to manipulate their own clothes as soon as possible. Of course, at this age, your child will naturally be more dependent on you than older children would be. It's a good thing to remember.

PROMPTING

Your child is going to need you more than an older child would. You will prompt on those easy catches I've referred to several times. You must keep in mind that *you* will be responsible for your child peeing more than the parent of a two-year-old would be. Your child *will* get it and *will* eventually initiate, but they will need more help.

Charlene, a mom I once worked with, figured out her nineteen-month-old would say "up." Charlene thought she wanted to be carried. She was half right: her daughter wanted to be carried to the potty. It took Charlene only two times of being peed on before she figured it out.

USING A LITTLE POTTY CHAIR

Companies that specialize in elimination communication gear have very small potties available. These should be easy for your child either to sit on or back themselves onto. It's pretty vital to have a little chair available. I often get some version of this: "We don't really like the little potty chair. We prefer he learn right on the big toilet, since that's where he'll be going." That's okay, I guess, but my question is, "Don't you want him to be able to go on his own?"

Until your child can physically maneuver onto the big toilet safely, they're going to need your help. I think it's well worth the twenty dollars to get the little potty. Soon enough, they'll move to the big toilet. But if they have the notion to go on their own, we certainly want to make it easy for them to do so.'

A LONGER PROCESS FOR THE YOUNGER CHILD

This will not necessarily be harder, but it may be longer. That the progress can be slower is okay. Just don't expect it to be done in a week. I find that to be pretty rare. The thing to look for is progress, not perfection. As long as you see consistent progress, it's all good. A more realistic time line is about two to three weeks.

BE REALLY READY TO TELL EVERYONE TO FRICK OFF

If you know in your gut that your kid is capable of this and you feel ready, *go for it*. But society is going to tell you up, down, and sideways that you are crazy. I do not think this is so. I congratulate you on your intuition! Fabulous. Rock on and don't look back. My mother tells the story of me being so, so late to potty train that she was embarrassed to leave the house with me. I was twenty-four months. That's how much we've societally shifted the expected age of this milestone.

You will start the plan just as I laid it out in chapter 5, "Ditch the Diapers! The How-To." Always remember that the goal is to move along the time line from Clueless, to I Peed, to I'm Peeing, to I Have to Go Pee. Each little component may take a bit of time. It's all good as long as you feel progress.

Be aware that the child under twenty months may not be getting it for a while before it clicks. You can still potty train a young child who is a little clueless, but it will take longer, and it's really going to be on you. If you work outside the home and don't have a willing care provider, you should probably wait. I would say that a month is a realistic time frame for progressing through the time line. Does a month sound too long to you? Then wait. But if it sounds amazing that in one small month you'll be done with diapers, then proceed.

My first attempt at training Pascal was at eighteen months. At the time, I was a single mom (still am), I owned a clothing store, and his day care was very unwilling (they thought he was much too young). Within a day of potty training, I knew it wasn't clicking. I was bummed because I knew it was possible for him, but in my life at that time, it would have brought more stress. I let it go and he potty trained in a matter of days when he was twenty-two months.

You don't know what kind of potty trainee you have until you jump in and go for it. At this age, if it's not going according to plan, you can always rediaper, and it will not hurt the process one bit. There is a lot going on developmentally before twenty months, and your child just may not have the skill set. If you feel able to be there and help, that's awesome. I'm not trying to scare you or be a big bummer, but I want to be realistic with you.

Older Than Thirty-Six Months

I really do recommend potty training within the twenty- to thirty-month range. I push this out to thirty-six months because that's still okay. If you go past that, you might run into a few potential problems.

There are a few reasons why you might have waited until this age. The top one is you just didn't know. Our societal norm keeps getting older and older, and it's not uncommon to see four- and four-and-a-half-year-olds not potty trained. Another typical reason for waiting until this age is that you gave it a solid shot at a younger age and were met with too many struggles and decided to rediaper and "wait till they're ready." And the next big reason is that your child has some sort of delay (e.g., speech, developmental, gross motor) or other diagnosis and you decided to back-burner potty training.

Typically, upon reading this, I have parents who freak out that they've waited too long. I also see parents riddled with guilt that they haven't done this yet. Listen to me: neither of these feelings will serve you. I am sure you are an excellent parent who really thought you were doing what's best for your child and your family. There's no reason to feel guilt or shame or to freak out. It's all going to be okay; you just need to be prepared for a different set of potential problems.

THE THREE BIGGEST PITFALLS
Deadlines

One of the biggest issues with potty training a child over thirty-six months is that there is most likely a deadline looming. In most cases, it's preschool, a program, or a camp that you've already booked and paid for and they only accept fully-potty-trained children. Or maybe you've been doing the whole "waiting till they're ready" but you're seeing nothing—no signs of interest or readiness—and you notice time is ticking away and you might need to push this along. The deadline itself isn't the problem; it's waiting until you're pushed up against it that gets troublesome.

Every August, I get frantic parents contacting me that they have a week to fully potty train their three-year-old or they can't go to preschool. Please don't do this. If you have a looming deadline for potty training, give yourself a few months' leeway. You want your child to have more than enough time to really solidify this skill. The other big issue is that if you push right up against that deadline, you'll be a mess. You'll be future-tripping (worried about next week and not being in the present moment). You'll put too much pressure on your child who will feel this and almost assuredly rebel and show lots of resistance. Too much pressure is the number one killer of potty training.

Personality

Somewhere close to three years old, your child goes through individuation, the process by which they realize that they are separate from you. This is the age of free will, choice, and the word *NO*. The popular term *threenager* comes from the idea that teenagers go through a similar process with higher stakes—though I would argue against the notion that this stage is marked by what seems like contentious behavior.

I call it "blossoming personality," and it's developmentally appropriate, but it can be wearing on you and your nerves. It's the age of you saying the sky is blue only to be met with, "NO! It's pink!" It's the age of wanting to do for themselves and not yet being able. This blossoming personality means that potty training can be wrought with power struggles. I have never met a typical three-year-old who needs to be made aware of peeing and pooping. They are never clueless. Potty training most often becomes about managing their personality and not actually learning how to use the potty. Now many people do wait until three or older and say their kids just did it on their own. But through all my work, I've learned that's a total crapshoot and they got lucky. For most kids, this age can be more difficult because in the power struggle, they hold the power: their own pee and poop.

Habit

Diaper wearing is just a habit we're trying to break. The longer your child is in one, the more entrenched the habit is. Is it easier to break a two-year habit or a four-year habit? I mention this because this is a place where you might get frustrated with your child, but it's also a place in which you should have lots of grace. The diaper is all they've ever known, and we're asking them to give up something that makes them very comfortable. I mention this because a lot of parents think the child is being difficult, but really we might have to lean in with a little more love and grace.

Back to the Beginning

Those are the three biggest pitfalls you need to be aware of. Regardless of how old or where you are in the progress of prior attempts, you should ALWAYS go back to the beginning with block 1. Sometimes parents buck up against me with this idea. They feel they've made *some* good headway and don't want to take any steps backward. I have to tell you, though, straight up, if you're struggling with potty training over the age of three, you're not almost there. There's a problem somewhere along the line, and the only way to tell what that is is to start at the beginning.

A former client, Mary, came to me because her son, Dillon, was thirty-eight months and was being denied admission to a preschool because he wasn't fully toilet trained. Dillon could pee on the potty most of the time, but poop was hit or miss. Sometimes he'd do it in his pants, sometimes make it to the potty. He was still having a few pee accidents as well. Sometimes he was wildly resistant to the potty, and other times he'd just go. It looked like a mess, and Mary was going crazy because of the preschool thing. It was, like, *serious*.

When I recommended she go back to that first naked day she really fought me. She didn't think he needed to go back. She believed that he had made enough progress that he didn't need to go backward. But in a case like this and maybe in yours, *we need to know where it went wrong*. You can't go back and fix something if you don't know what went wrong in the first place. And clearly something went wrong. It's about going back and getting those blocks of learning, those phases, rock solid and playing around with them if they are not.

In short, Mary did go back and did the progression of block 1, and it clicked for Dillon. We never did get an "aha!" as to what went wrong. It wasn't very clear to either of us. But just going back and doing it all in order made it work for Dillon.

The same thing happens with whatever struggles you are having with potty training. I don't know what went wrong, and I'm guessing you don't know either, so just start over. The parts they've gotten down pat will just be review. And as with Mary, I wouldn't look for some big "aha!" I've done this with thousands of kids, and I know, know, know this progression works.

So that's your first task. The next big thing is what to do with power struggles. The best way to end a power struggle is to let go of your end of the rope. You will never, ever win a power struggle with a toddler. They are made of steel and don't give AF. So you give this responsibility for the learning to them: "All right, Jamie, so how the eff do I do that?" You don't argue. You don't cajole. You don't beg or negotiate. And you never, ever let them smell your fear.

You begin that first day with, "We have not done a good job with potty training, so I'm going to help you learn it the right way. You're going to help by letting me know when you have to pee or by going yourself. There's the little potty or the big toilet. You can choose." *Most kids are really waiting for you to show up with the consistency.* I'm not saying that's always the case, but often it is. So here you are, waiting for them, and all this time they've been waiting on you. I know . . . f**k. It's okay.

If, during that day, you are met with resistance, you continue to back off. For instance, use that throwaway prompt, "You have to pee; there's your potty." *You must leave room for them to make the good decision themselves.* This could take a day or two, so be patient. You want to dance along the delicate line between prompting and backing off.

For most parents, that's going to be enough. Time after time, I've seen parents shocked at how quickly and easily it went with a former potty monster. Often I think it's a matter of the consistency and going back and learning. If a kid doesn't get all the components of a process (like potty training), they tend to stop caring. I call it the "inner f**k it," which is basically them saying, "I suck at this, so

I'm not going to try." Our kids *want* to do well. They *want* to do the right thing. We have to believe that. A lot of resistance in the older kid is because they haven't learned something quite the right way. We want to assume your child is just missing a component.

Time and time again, once we show up with firm but loving boundaries, the child does fine or at least so much better.

A lot of times parents abandon earlier attempts at potty training because of behavior or poop withholding, so prepare yourself by going over chapters 10 and 13 again. If you are anticipating a struggle and you can swing it, a consultation would be super helpful. Also, be sure to see the questions near the end of this book in chapter 17.

The bottom line is that potty training can be done at any age, regardless of my recommended time frame. Just be aware that under twenty months usually means a longer learning curve and isn't suited for most kids in day care. And over thirty months, you're looking at very little learning that has to be done but potentially lots more undesirable behavior with all the blossoming personality.

CHAPTER 15

The Reset

I've coined the term *reset* for those instances in which, for whatever reason, you need a do-over. An erase. A start again. It means you rediaper your child and forgo all things potty and potty training. There are a couple of caveats however, so let's dig in.

The reset can be used only once. It is NO GOOD if used more than once. Let's remember that for many kids, the diaper is all they have known and they prefer it. If you repeatedly start and have to give up, that's what your child will learn, and the potty training process will become infinitely harder. I used to think there was an optimal length of time, but it really depends on your schedule. I have found the most challenging aspect of how long you should reset is busy schedules and carving out a good amount of time to retackle potty training.

The best way to tell if you need a reset is if you are at the end of your rope, maybe even crying, or when you're banging your head against the wall over and over expecting different results. I don't mean you're feeling the normal exhaustion and frustration that the first few days of potty training can bring. Rather, the reset is for those who have given it their all, and I do mean *all*. I want your child potty trained, but I also want you sane and your home harmonious. If you are feeling strung out, a little insane, and you've been cleaning pee off the floor for more than two weeks, consider a reset. If your entire life revolves around trying to figure out when this kid is going to let their pee loose and you have no other thoughts besides potty training, consider a reset.

There are three major times to do a reset:

1. *Before using this book*: You tried potty training in any way, shape, or form, and you have a disaster on your hands or even just a hot mess. Then you heard from a friend about my book and you ran to buy it. You are gung-ho to start, but you have this writhing mess on your hands. *Reset.*

2. *After getting this book and giving it a really solid effort*: Either your child never got it or got it and their behavior suddenly flipped and they're crazy every time you mention the potty. It also looks like a hot mess, and you cannot figure out what happened. *Reset.*

3. *You are crying or are totally beside yourself*: You cannot be a good teacher if you're emotionally all over the map. *Reset.*

The reset should never be used with a child over three. If you refer to chapter 14, "Younger Than Twenty Months, Older Than Thirty-Six Months," you will see that any child over that age who's not getting it is most likely showing *behavior*, not a glitch in learning, and that won't be resolved with more time.

The reasoning behind the reset is that it gives you and your household a big breather. We need you sane to be effective. If you are crying over potty training, there's no way you are going to be able to keep firm and consistent. You will slip into bribery and negotiation. I know this. Much like a torturer, your toddler *will* break you, and you'll be scattered, which sends the signal that you are not in control. If you are not in control, your child is. And that's unsafe for your child.

The other thing the reset does is give your child a breather. Potty training is a lot to learn. But if there's too much of a struggle, they'll get stuck in a rut. Just as during a tantrum, nothing can be learned from this place. If your child is stuck in a rut, there's no point in continuing. The days where there are fights are not days that count toward good potty training. Nothing was learned.

Finally, the reset lets your toddler "win" a little bit, which is a good thing. It can settle things and make the next effort calmer.

Or perhaps you are not getting resistance, just utter cluelessness from your child, and you wonder whether a reset is warranted. In such a case, you have to be the judge. Utter cluelessness for more than a week is something I have never seen in a neurotypical, average child. I've seen kids not want to deal with the potty or pretend it doesn't exist, but that's not cluelessness. That's passive resistance and should be worked through.

So how do you handle a reset?

First, you rediaper. I'd prefer you do this at night before bed and just continue doing so in the morning. The one thing I'd want to avoid is returning to diapers in the middle of a fit of resistance. If your child is screaming and you say, "Fine! Put a diaper on!," this will send the wrong message.

The message you want to send is this: "We're having a hard time with this so we're going to all calm down a bit." You can often just put a diaper back on without much fanfare. This isn't meant as punishment or giving in. This is merely to regroup.

Second, you put away the potty chair, and you don't say boo about potty training. You will most likely get one of the following reactions:

> Nothing. No mention of it, and you actually can sense relief in your child.
>
> Your child asks about it but doesn't ask to use it. Use the statement above, and then change the subject. This is not the time to lecture about their misuse of the potty.
>
> Your child suddenly, for the first time, asks to use the potty.
> I'll get to this one in another minute.

Third, you breathe normally for the first time in a long time. You most likely will have the experience of "having your kid back." Enjoy this time. Don't linger in the past or be freaked out by the future. It is what it is, and it's meant to be a time of regrouping and regaining harmony.

Fourth, set a new date. This is vital. Otherwise, time will slip through your fingers and a year will go by. I've seen it happen. Your child will be marinating on all you have taught them thus far. It won't all go out the window, I promise you. Hold that date in your thoughts, and you can even throw it out there casually a few times: "You are not using the potty properly, so we put it away. Don't worry, we'll start again next month [or whenever]." Do this casually so your child knows it's coming.

Now, if your child asks to use the potty and it does seem like they will use it correctly, you can give them *one shot*. You can either take the potty out or you can use the insert. If your child does indeed use the potty the right way, you can tell them, "Thank you. I will leave the potty out for you. If you don't use it, it goes away again for a while." If there is even one time they do not use it properly, you need to follow through with the reset, no matter what they say. This *cannot* become a game: it's either use the potty or don't use the potty. The biggest problem is they're deciding to use it sometimes, and that's going to add a lot of time and mixed messages to this process.

If your child is over three, you will not want to use the reset. However, if your child is under twenty-two months, you may want to do a reset, but you will go about it differently. For the child under this age, there is a very real possibility that they are clueless. There's a lot going on developmentally, and the timing may just be off. Don't use this as a cop-out. I have seen sixteen-month-olds who potty train with no problem. If you want to potty train between sixteen and twenty-two months, that is awesome. Chances are your child has shown some indication that this is possible. Go with your intuition. You should have a sense of progress. If you see *no* progress, consider a reset. I also think it's great to try at this younger age because you never know if you have a little rock star on your hands until you start. Might as well give it a whirl and see, and there's lots of wiggle room for a reset if not.

For this younger child, you do not need to put the potty away. If they indicate that they'd like to use the potty, it's fine. With this age, there's usually little to no behavior going on. The child is just not connecting the dots. You still want to set a new start date for when you'll try again, and keep that in your head so diapers don't take over.

Just to be clear, from twenty-two to twenty-four months is an unclear zone. Sometimes a child can be truly clueless and sometimes not. It's your call. I would look back on their other milestones and see if they were on target or early or late. That's usually the best indicator.

Two things often happen when parents read this chapter or feel they might need a reset. The first is that I'll hear from a parent who's at the end of their rope on the second day of potty training and wants to know if a reset is appropriate. But that's a ridiculously small amount of time in which to lose your marbles. Your child is learning a new skill, and no other major milestone has been achieved in so short a time frame. This is your child, and *you* have the magic. Adjust, get creative, and think about what might be going on. There's a fair amount of thinking on your feet about your particular child needed here.

The second reaction I get is massive resistance to the reset—an overwhelming sense of *No way.* The parents feel that the reset would be a massive backslide. Many parents will point to the one pee they got in the potty in the last three days. "She did it once! See?" To which I say, "Listen. I truly believe in most instances that working through the problems is the best way to potty train. But one pee on the potty in three days in week two of potty training is not progress. You are stuck. The only way to get unstuck is to change something." I'm sure you've heard the Einstein quote: "The definition of insanity is doing the same thing over and over again, expecting different results."

Chances are that by the time you are considering a reset, you have tried many different things. For whatever reason, it's not working. Sometimes it's absolutely clear, and sometimes you'll never know exactly why. But we do need to shake things up a bit, and that's what the reset does. It shakes things up and calms them down. While you are figuring out what might have gone wrong or what you could change, and at the same time you are still potty training and are getting nothing but pee on the floor, you are going to go insane. Insane parents are wildly ineffective teachers.

As I mentioned at the beginning of the chapter, the reset is good for before or after starting this book but NOT BOTH. Let's say that you have a child who's twenty-eight months. You've given potty training a pretty good attempt, not using my book, and now you don't have a potty-trained kid but you don't have a disaster either. You finally bought my book to seal the deal. If you don't have a disaster, I'd jump right in with that first day. Many times I hear, "I think she was just waiting for ME to be consistent." Or you can choose a start date in two weeks and rediaper them until then.

If you have read this book because you *do* have a disaster, absolutely reset your child before beginning again. You've got a massive whiteboard with a bunch of squiggles on it, and it's time to erase and start over.

Once again, it's impossible for me to know your exact situation. I trust your intuition, and you should do the same. You know your child best. Weigh your options and see what feels right to you.

The reset is good just once. Otherwise, you will teach your child that if they pitch a big enough fit, you will cave and use diapers, and for many kids, that's what they want. I think we can all agree that this is a disaster in the making.

CHAPTER 16

Special Circumstances, including Delays and Neurodiversity

In every potty training journey, there are going to be special circumstances. Sometimes these occur once you begin the actual process but other times, these may be factors that have made you wait before even attempting potty training. Let's dive into the most common special circumstances that I've seen over the years and how to approach them.

Extreme Fear of the Potty

Some children may appear to be extremely afraid of the potty. This used to be rare to see in my work, but in recent years there has been a tremendous uptick.

First, you need to ascertain that this truly is fear—not resistance and not the usual minor fear a child will show at doing something new. One mom equated the appearance of "true fear" with that of a cat being stuffed into a small bucket of water. If your child looks something like that, the fear is real, and it's there from the start. Most often it appears that although these kids are afraid of the actual potty, in reality, they are typically afraid of the "free" release of pee or poop. We go back to that feeling that they've grown used to: containment. Their pee and poop have stayed close to their bodies, and that's what they are used to. No words or calm will help this child, and this isn't behavior.

The number one thing to remember is that this child will be able to learn nothing as long as they're in this place of fear, so don't even bother to try. If you seem to have a truly fearful child (and you will know for sure within a couple of days), then you need to approach potty training differently. You are going to move ahead much more slowly, and contrary to all I've said elsewhere in the book, you're going to take a casual approach. I've listed the casual plan in chapter 18 for you to follow. Not to worry, this still can be done in a timely manner.

Preemies

If your child was premature by more than four weeks, spent any significant time in the neonatal intensive care unit, or had trouble bonding, potty training could be delayed. However, this is not necessarily so, and by "delayed," I mean it might come closer to thirty months than twenty months. I'm not saying to wait until they're four or five. Preemies tend to be slightly behind their peers in other areas as well. Look at other milestones, and if all were a bit delayed, factor that into potty training. Do this not as an excuse to wait too long but to give your child the time they need to "catch up." Most kids I've worked with in this category are all caught up by twenty-four months. I usually go with adjusted age, and if that age falls within my recommended range, I say go for it.

Adoption

If you have adopted a child, particularly from another country, you should focus on forming a bond before beginning potty training. I once had a mom attend my class, and it turns out that her adopted daughter came to her quite bruised. Due to a lack of staff, the orphanage would tie the children to the potty until they produced. Obviously, this child did not need to start potty training anytime soon. I have never seen an adopted child have any problems with potty training, so I wouldn't give it any thought except to say not to rush it. If you adopted your child at a very young age, you can proceed with training as I've described with no problem.

When I first met Mona, she had just adopted her son who was twenty months old. He was bright and seemed capable and ready to potty train. We both suspected potty training had been started in his native country. But it didn't click, and after a few days he started to show fear around the potty. We decided that given the huge transition he'd been through, it would be best to go about training as I describe in the casual plan in chapter 18. Within a month, he was potty trained. Mona was thrilled because even though it took longer than she had originally hoped, it was still pretty wonderful to have him using the potty consistently. A recent adoption is a *major* transition, as is potty training itself. Go with your gut and your parental intuition.

Speech and Developmental Delays

If your child has been diagnosed with emotional or developmental delays, potty training *could* be delayed. I say "diagnosed" because every child develops differently, and while you may think something is up, it doesn't necessarily mean delayed. I know kids who haven't said a word until they were three and then became chatterboxes. I sometimes see parents use this as an excuse: "Well, he's not really delayed, but he doesn't do such and such . . . I don't know if he's ready to potty train." If other milestones have been met in a timely manner, I'd go for it. Obviously, the severity of the delay will dictate when potty training should begin. This is best discussed with your occupational therapist and any team you have in place. I would simply ask, "Is there any reason Johnny can't start potty training?" For example, if the delay is just in language, there's no reason he couldn't. But if the delay is in processing information, then things may not bode well for potty training until later.

Just because your child is delayed doesn't mean you have to forgo potty training. If anything, we'd like to give them every opportunity to learn and grow. Again, it's best for the parent to discuss their particular situation with the child's care team and see what limitations may affect the child. Be wary, however. My experience is that regardless of what the delay might be, children do best the earlier potty training begins. You may be advised to pick your battles, which is fair. But potty training often gets put on the back burner, and then you have a five-year-old in diapers. The reality is that you are going to make sure your child has the proper speech therapy or occupational therapy. But don't just let potty training go by the wayside. It will get harder with each year.

Neurodivergent Kids

Let's dive into neurodivergent kids, including those with autism spectrum disorder (ASD), attention deficit hyperactivity disorder (ADHD), or Down syndrome. These kids are awesome. Their brains may work differently but that doesn't mean they're any less capable. Let me be clear about a few things before we get started. This book is a guideline: you should always run it through the filter of your own child, take what you need, and leave the rest. I will always be staunch in my belief that you are the expert on your child. Professionals, doctors, and diagnoses are there to help you along your path, but you know your child best.

Throughout all my years of potty training, I have worked with many neurodivergent kids, and I've never seen the exact same issues in every child. Your child has a unique flair and flavor; this is true for all kids, but especially when we're looking at neurodivergent kids. How their diagnosis presents is different for each one. Yes, there are some broad strokes we can apply to the process, but I can never give you absolute, universal truths that would apply to every neurodivergent child. And if you find anyone who says they can, you should run.

Typically what happens is that most kids won't get an official diagnosis until around four or five, but most likely you've had a feeling that your child is not developing in a typical way. Maybe it's no eye contact, or maybe they're not hitting the milestones. Maybe it's just a gut feeling. I've never met a parent whose child gets a diagnosis and is totally surprised. But because your child is somehow presenting as "behind," potty training can get back-burnered because you've got bigger fish to fry here.

One of the issues I see come up with neurodivergent kids (particularly those on the autism spectrum) is that these kids struggle with change and big transitions. They also thrive under extreme consistency. So the longer they are in the habit of diaper wearing, the harder it can be to transition to the potty. I always recommend still beginning potty training between two and three years old. I also understand that this may not have been a priority for you or you were advised that your child isn't capable and so maybe you waited and now they are closer to four or even five. It's okay; you just need to be aware that the transition might be harder.

If you already have a team in place for your child, I'd ask them (especially the occupational therapist) if there's any reason your child couldn't potty train right now. Phrasing it like that will give you a better answer than simply asking if it's cool to potty train. Many doctors will give you a negative answer. But I know from my work that parents with a gut feeling and a mission can prove them wrong. Knowing where there might be a weakness is simply data to help you help your child. I also highly recommend starting potty training with a potty training consultant. There are several on my website who specialize in neurodivergent kids.

I know that's not always possible for every family, so we'll start with those broad strokes—things that are true for almost all neurodivergent kids. I worked on this with Liz Hansen, who's an Oh Crap! certified consultant and she works wonders with neurodivergent kids, particularly tough cases.

First and foremost, embrace the chaos and choose the joy. It's so easy to see where our kids might be lacking or where their differences lie. But there's much joy there as well. I encourage staying on the joy side of the street as much as you can. The next big thing is that Google is not your friend with potty training, especially if you haven't gotten an official diagnosis but are suspecting something is out of the ordinary. Google will send you down some dark rabbit holes. So connect with your child and choose your people wisely.

These are what we've found to be true with most kids. Again, these are not laws or absolutes but will help you tailor all the guidelines in this book to your particular child. We'll break down what we've found to be true about ADHD kids first. Some or all of this might apply to other neurodivergence too.

KIDS WITH ADHD AND ASD

Always allow for more time for potty training. Expect this to take closer to nine to fourteen days. Moreover, you should keep the potty in one spot; however, it is super helpful to have several in the common areas. These kids tend to be sensitive to the potty "chasing them," and it jacks up their nervous system.

With the average, neurotypical child, we see a pee dance and know it's time to sit. With ADHD kids, especially in the beginning, you don't want to make them sit just because you see the pee dance. The pee dance should, however, put you on high alert. Wait until you see the first actual drops of pee and then get them to the potty.

IPads and tablets are very useful for regulating neurodivergent kids. You should never take these away as a consequence. Not only is it not cool to do that to a kid who might need it, but it will also backfire on you. What you CAN do is make it a natural consequence: "There's pee on the floor and on your hands, so we need to put the iPad away so I can clean it " and, "If there's going to be poop on your hands, I'll have to put the iPad away."

There's a widespread rumor that ADHD kids can't nighttime potty train. This is not true. What IS true is that the antidiuretic hormone, released with melatonin and dictated by the circadian rhythm, often isn't released because ADHD kids tend to have flipped circadian rhythms. These are the kids who might appear to be night owls. Unless you plan on living a feral, wild life that doesn't rely on any societal norms (and it's cool if you do), this is something that needs attending to. This might be okay if you plan on your child never entering school, but otherwise you need to have a strict routine to help them keep their circadian rhythm in a healthy zone. In other words, they can't be night owls if they're going to go to school; they will be too tired. A normal bedtime of around 7:00 or 7:30 is vital. You can assist them by making sure they get good morning sunlight (and sunsets too) and a lot of big play during the day. There's a great deal of information online about helping the circadian rhythm so I'll leave that to you. One other important thing about nighttime training is that these kids MUST be bare-bummed. Commando with PJ bottoms isn't enough.

When we work with autistic kids (with both high needs of support and lower), many of the same things apply as with ADHD. One thing is clear: you need to reduce your talking to a minimum. Most kids with these diagnoses don't need extra stimuli.

One of the first things to determine is whether your little one is more of a sensory seeker or a sensory avoider. Most ASD kids have some sort of sensory issue, and while it's not always one or the other, we do find that one of these leads most of the time. If your child tends to the sensory seeking, use ample touch while on the potty and in general. If they are more of a sensory avoider, use as few stimuli as possible—for example, no talking, no tablets, probably even no reading or singing, among others.

In addition, you don't want to put them on the potty at timed intervals, say every thirty minutes. While this is aggravating to almost all kids, it's especially dysregulating for ASD kids. If they do not release relatively quickly, do not make them stay on the potty. Avoid using any entertainment while using the potty. A helpful tool is a bubble timer, a visual representation of what's happening when the poop comes out. It can also serve as an actual timer so you don't overdo the sitting and trying. And it's also calming for sensory kids.

Many people make a pictorial poster of all the steps used in going to the potty. Although it can be helpful for some kids, in general, I find it's overkill. What IS really useful is a pictorial poster of the general schedule of the day and a handmade picture flip book not just for the potty. When making a poster or book of the schedule, extreme consistency is essential. These kids thrive on extreme consistency. They can have inflexible thinking, and schedules help them cope. Of course, things can and do change suddenly, so giving them a huge heads-up can be helpful.

Prompts to use the potty should always be tied into another scheduled activity—for example, potty and then lunch. Potty and then tablet. Potty and then snack. You should reduce prompting down to about five times a day. These kids tend to be highly sensitive to overprompting. The more you can tie these to another activity or regularly scheduled thing, the better.

I've also learned that keeping the potty chair next to something stable helps immensely, for example a couch. I'm unsure if that's for stability or a level of privacy, but it's definitely a dial mover. Beyond that, there's so much about your child's personality and quirks that it would be hard to give more specifics. Lean into the child you know and love and your parental intuition.

DOWN SYNDROME

I've worked with many children with Down syndrome. I do hear from parents that word on the street is that they are hard to potty train, but this has not been my experience. Again, I think what probably happens is there's a lot going on at potty training age. Potty training doesn't take precedence in these situations, so most parents tend to do it at a much later age, when they are dealing with a more entrenched habit that is harder to break.

I have no specifics that are out of my normal recommendations except to expect a slightly longer learning curve, probably more like two weeks. Since kids with Down syndrome tend to have low muscle tone, poop can be harder to pass. Be sure that your child is pooping with ease before starting potty training. Some parents use stool softeners to ensure success. And as with any neurodivergence, hiring a consultant can ease your mind with one-on-one support through this process.

ALL OTHER MEDICAL ISSUES

I've worked with thousands of kids with a myriad of issues. We use this book as a base and tweak it once I get to know the child and whatever they are presenting with. I'm not just trying to blow you off when I say working with a consultant is best. No matter what, every kid has strengths that we can work with and every kid has an "in." In most instances, this is the best way to ensure your sanity and their success.

Regardless of what diagnosis your child has, no matter what issues you are facing, lead with trust. Trust that your child is much more capable than you know, so trust unless proven otherwise. You already probably have the tools to work with whatever your child is presenting with. You can apply those to this process as well.

Major Transitions

Any major transition can cause a regression, a backward step. In potty training, this means your accident-free child suddenly starts having lots of them. Most often, you hear about regression when a family is expecting another child, but any major transition can cause a regression.

Moving and divorce are two major transitions that are very stressful no matter what kind of game face you have on. Your child absolutely feels your stress even if you think you don't say or do anything to express what you are feeling. Children are remarkably intuitive. They live and breathe by our energy.

Stress and tension may be unavoidable, and it's best to say things out loud in terms they can understand, for example, "You know, Mommy and Daddy are having a hard time right now. Can you feel it? But it's okay. We're going to figure out how to do what's best for our family." "You know, I'm really nervous about moving. Are you? And I've been so busy packing and getting ready, maybe I haven't been spending enough time with you. Let's play something."

Don't bring up any regression during these conversations. Your goal is to talk about the big, pink elephant in the house, not the symptoms you're all experiencing.

Many parents are afraid to hit this dead-on, but I think it's best to have this conversation. Children are feeling the tension or the stress, and if we don't help them express that, they will continue to act out in strange ways. Remember that acting out isn't bad. It means something is happening internally for the child, and they don't have the words to express it.

This is an opportunity to let your child express their feelings. Once you open the door, you'll be amazed at what children will say. Just giving big topics attention will resolve a lot of accidents and other forms of acting out. Be careful, however, to not make promises you can't keep. Talk and ask questions, even if it feels that they are too young to understand. You can be sure that the information is getting in.

One final thought on regressions is that you should not put a diaper back on your child! Once your child is potty trained or even in the beginning stages, putting a diaper on them says one thing only: "I don't trust you. I'm telling you all day how I know you can do it and I have confidence in you. But really, I don't trust you." This is extremely damaging to the whole process. If you don't trust your child, they will never trust themselves.

And for the billionth time as well: your energy, your vibe, your nonverbal cues are leading the show here. Be sure and be steady.

CHAPTER 17

Random Tips and Questions

TEETHING

Beware the two-year molars. If your child suddenly starts having accidents, it could be teething. Teething the two-year molars, based on my own observation, is hell. While all sorts of preteething goes on, when the teeth actually break the surface of the gums is the worst for your child. It can bring fevers, diarrhea, and really "off" behavior. Do whatever it is you do to manage the pain, and do your best to maintain the status quo.

GETTING SICK A COUPLE OF DAYS INTO POTTY TRAINING

It's bizarre how often a kid will get sick a day or two into potty training. If it's a minor cold or is otherwise bearable in general, try to muddle through and expect just to stay afloat. If the sickness is not minor and your child is lethargic or bed-bound, it's okay to re-diaper and start fresh when they are themselves again. They won't learn anything while they are sick anyway, so it almost doesn't count. Under these circumstances, rediapering doesn't damage the process at all. Most kids seem to recognize that they aren't capable when they're ill. We also want your child focused on resting and healing, not learning.

TRAVEL IN THE EARLY STAGES OF POTTY TRAINING

Many people have to travel soon into potty training or live in remote areas where it's a long way to go grocery shopping. Depending on how your child is doing—and you will have a good sense of this about a week in—you have a few options. It's perfectly acceptable to use a "travel diaper." I would call it that so your child understands it's out of the norm—it's a "just in case." If you choose to use a travel diaper, put it on the last minute before leaving and take it off immediately upon arrival. You should also try your hardest to honor any pee calls even if your child is wearing the diaper. The travel diaper is especially useful for long plane rides. This is because traveling with a toddler is stressful enough, never mind having to keep a keen eye on the potty situation. Everything is better when your stress level is kept hovering around sane.

POTTY TRAINING WITH SIBLINGS

Potty training your first is somewhat easier in that you can focus on that one child and that's it. It gets a little stickier when you're potty training your second, third, etc. because of course you've got other kids to attend to. I see the most difficulties going from your first to your second child because I think that's the biggest change. Once you have two kids, the transition to three or more seems easier. When you have siblings in the mix, try your best to time potty training on school break. This will give you plenty of time but also eliminate school/day care drop offs for the older child. I'd also try to coordinate starting on a weekend so your spouse can be available to help.

Depending on how old the sibling is, they can often be helpful. They can show the younger kid the ropes, or maybe help with getting snacks and playing so you can keep a keen eye. Or potentially, the older child can stay at a friend's or grandma's house for the weekend. You know your kids best so this is your call.

Be sure the older child is getting some extra attention during this time. Maybe when the younger is napping or you and your spouse can tag team kids. A lot of older siblings feel the weight of you paying so much attention to the younger one.

If you do need to leave the house for the older child's needs and the younger one isn't quite there yet with potty training, it's okay to use a diaper for the car. Peeing in the car seat is a big mess and using a diaper for a car ride to school or an activity isn't going to kill the process. However, be mindful that this isn't a significant portion of the day. It should be used for car rides and that's it.

DON'T FORGET TO PLAN AHEAD

For the first day or two of potty training, you must keep your eyes on your child allll the time. So, don't forget to plan ahead. The night before you can cut up fruit, veggies, cheese cubes . . . whatever you plan on feeding your little one, be sure to have it pretty ready to just take out and eat.

Roughly plan out some activities for your child so you don't lose your mind. The first day can be especially boring for you and you may draw a blank in the moment. Write down all the things your child likes to do and keep the list on the fridge for easy reminding.

You don't have to do anything special or out of the ordinary. I'd have Play-Doh on hand, art supplies, sensory bins, puzzles, maybe a few new sticker books. Nothing crazy out of the ordinary but more a reminder for you if you have a brain fart mid-day and forget everything your kid likes to do.

HIRING OUT THE POTTY TRAINING

Don't be afraid to enlist help. I had a mom take my class and then I ran into her a month later. I asked her how it went and she said, "Fantastic. I hired my babysitter to do it. My daughter is totally potty trained." Hire it out if you want to! Most of the time this works extremely well because others aren't nearly as invested as we the parents are. There's no shame in getting help.

SWIM DIAPERS

These are fine in the early stages of potty training. The circumstances around swimming are special enough that using them doesn't create confusion and won't derail the process. What will derail the process is having your child be the one who poops in the pool, and everyone has to get out, and all eyes are on you, and not in a good way. Just put the diaper on your child at the same time as the swimsuit, and be sure to get a pee before getting into the pool and when you get out.

The same goes for the beach and lake. Use your judgment, though. If you have a beach house and are spending eight hours a day on the beach, you don't want them in a swim diaper the whole time. You should encourage your child to get out of the water if they feel the need to pee or poop. And you should honor this request as if there weren't a diaper on. I know it can be inconvenient, but you are not using a diaper for convenience. You are using it so a big glaring accident doesn't ruin your life for a day.

MY PEDIATRICIAN SAID TO WAIT UNTIL SHE'S READY

I have had many pediatricians among my clients. In fact, many years ago, when some pediatricians used my services, they asked me to give them copies of my book for their waiting rooms. It's kind of how my book got on the map, really. When I switched my son's pediatrician and filled out all the registration paperwork, she noticed my email at Oh Crap! Potty Training and asked me about it. Then she asked for cards and brochures, saying, "I would love to have someone to direct my patients to! I don't potty train kids."

This makes perfect sense. Over the years, I've had innumerable clients tell me they tried to discuss potty troubles with their doctor and the doctor cut them off with, "Oh, just wait till they're ready," which is fine unless you *know* your kid is capable and just need some suggestions on how to get started or fix a problem you've encountered.

Here's the deal, straight up: always listen to your doctor. But doctors get paid to look for things that are wrong with your child. Doctors help your sick child get well and heal broken bones. They find ear infections and heart murmurs. And realistically, they have precious little time to spend hearing about your child's potty training struggles. I don't mean that as any sort of slight against doctors.

I think part of it is our health care system and the speed at which we need to be seen. I also think doctors tend to look at parents like we're whack jobs. Let's face it: we can all be a little crazy in the doctor's office. Okay—I can, at least.

Here are some sound bites from appointments with Pascal's pediatrician:

"How's he eating?" She's looking for general answers, not the blow-by-blow I want to give her.

"How are his stools?" She's looking for solid versus mushy, gray versus brown, not the minutiae I'd like to give her.

"He likes kindergarten?" She's looking for me to tell her that everything is normal, not every frigging cute thing he tells me every day.

So when the pediatrician asks if your child is potty training, she means it should be on your radar. She doesn't want to see a poop log. It's not a pediatrician's area of expertise, and they do not want it to be. The average pediatrician hasn't actually potty trained a variety of kids. Don't get me wrong—if you think there's a medical reason for your child's potty training troubles, *ask!!!* But don't expect solutions to nonmedical problems. Bottom line is that your pediatrician is busy with the job of keeping your child healthy and well. You can't expect them to know everything about everything.

PENISES AND POTTY TRAINING

I get a fair number of inquiries about the penis as it relates to potty training.

Standing to Pee

When do boys start to stand up to pee? The best time to start is when he's actually tall enough for his penis to clear the toilet bowl. When they're first potty trained, this isn't usually the case. You don't want to mess around with a step stool, a toddler, and a big porcelain bowl. When you start with the potty, have him sit on the potty chair or toilet insert. These sometimes come with a pee guard that I've never heard, even once, of working. The best thing to do is just tell him, "Hold your penis down." You can gently put his legs together to help him do this. Most boys don't mind touching their penises, so it shouldn't be a problem. When you start like this, it quickly becomes habit. When he is tall enough or old enough to reach the toilet with his penis while standing, you can have him push up on the skin right above the penis, as opposed to holding the penis for aim. This gives him a great amount of control and eliminates the whole "loaded fire hose in his hands" issue. Yes, once boys figure out they can hold it and aim, it does quickly become a game, so if you can stop that from the start, you'll be better off. I know some people suggest cereal in the toilet to practice aiming, but again, I think this just sets up the potential for a mess. Plus, it's pee. Do you really want to make a big game of it?

It's your call.

One thing I hear a lot is, "But he wants to pee just like his dad." Absolutely no offense, but this is kind of lame. Dad does tons of things that his boy can't do yet. You can simply say, "When you get a little bit bigger, then you can pee like Daddy." Don't make it an issue, and your child won't either.

Also, even at this young age, if there's dribble on the seat or bowl edge, teach him to wipe it off with some toilet paper. Future generations of women will thank you.

Circumcised versus Intact

Is there a difference in potty training for circumcised versus intact penises? No. The process is exactly the same. I have noticed that with the foreskin intact, the penis hangs down a bit more, which makes aiming a bit easier at first. Also, there have been questions as to whether the foreskin could hold a mini-reservoir of pee. Again, no. If you've got a dribbler, it's the kid, not the penis.

That's all I've got on penises. If you've got a random penis question, feel free to ask. I'd prefer it relate to potty training, but hey, I'm open to any random penis question. I can't say I'm an expert but . . . you know . . .

WHEN CAN I MOVE THE POTTY CHAIR TO THE BATHROOM?

This is a question I get asked a lot. It is totally your call. Usually it happens when you get sick of the potty chair being in the living room (or playroom or kitchen). A lot of this will depend on your house setup. There will be a moment when you know your child can make it to the bathroom. There's usually just a natural progression toward your child wanting privacy and/or knowing the bathroom is *the* place for the potty. If you are unsure about whether they can actually make it, keep the potty chair where it's handy. Don't put up barriers to their success.

WHEN CAN I SWITCH TO THE BIG TOILET?

Same goes for the switch to the big toilet and ditching the potty chair altogether. Over time, around a month or so after potty training, you should be regularly offering the big toilet over the little potty, and your child should start getting used to both. Most kids gravitate toward the toilet, again with that sense that it is the right place to be. If your child really loves the potty, it's okay. Eventually the infatuation fades. I've never, ever had a weird situation, like a five-year-old who will only use the little potty. Go with your gut.

WHEN CAN I GET RID OF THE INSERT?

Once again, same deal with the insert. It's just a matter of when your child is ready to let it go. Don't rush ditching the insert. Your child's bum isn't going to be big enough for the toilet seat for quite some time, and if they fall into the toilet, you can kiss all your hard work goodbye.

WHEN WILL THEY START WIPING THEIR OWN BUTT?

When you feel like you can deal with the crappy job they do of wiping their own butt. Kidding. No, I'm not. Once again, your call. You both will come to some agreement at some point. Just like teaching them to brush their teeth, start by taking turns, first them, then you. Very often this is a matter of logistics; little arms aren't actually able to reach around and find the actual poop. I've mentioned this earlier but I think it's really unrealistic to expect a three-year-old to do a good job wiping their own butt. Most kids begin to do a good job around five or six.

HOW SHOULD I SANITIZE THE POTTY CHAIR?

Do not use hard-core sanitizers on the potty chair; a baby wipe is fine. If you are using Clorox or something similar, your child may get a rash. This is particularly true of girls, whose vaginas tend to rub against the potty chair.

WHAT DOES "DONE" LOOK LIKE? HOW WILL I KNOW MY KID IS POTTY TRAINED?

There's no defined marker for "done" when it comes to potty training. Most children may have an accident or two after being "done." Our children are human. They can be unsure, scared, emotional, overjoyed—and any of these can bring on an accident. They can be teething, be feverish, have an ear infection, or be overtired. Any can bring on an accident. For me, I think "done" is when potty training fades into the fabric of your life. You will have to prompt occasionally, you will have to insist sometimes, you may have to change their clothes once in a while, but none of it will seem earth-shattering. For most moms, they mark "done" in their heads with potty success during increasingly challenging or exciting events. *Disney on Ice*: no accidents—woo-hoo!! Went to Grandma's for three days: no accidents—woo-hoo! Took a five-hour car ride: peed at the rest stops—woo-hoo! Like any other skill, your child's ability to use the potty gets better and better until you're no longer thinking about it ALL. THE. TIME. On the flip side, if your child is having an accident every single day, that's not "done." Go back and tighten the process. Run through the blocks of learning fast, and clean up the frayed edges a bit. And remember, don't let anyone else determine what "done" means to you and your family.

MY CHILD KEEPS TOUCHING THEMSELVES BECAUSE THEY'RE BARE-BOTTOMED.

It's normal and healthy exploration that can happen anytime a child is naked. You can remind them that there are certain times and places for this exploration. But this has nothing to do with potty training.

MY CHILD KEEPS TAKING OFF THEIR DIAPER, AND I DON'T KNOW WHAT TO DO.

I specialize in taking off the diaper, so I'm on your kid's team here. It's time to potty train and often this behavior is at night, so it's time to night train. All behavior is communication, so clearly your little one is communicating that they no longer want a diaper on.

I USED ELIMINATION COMMUNICATION, AND NOW I'M UNSURE HOW TO BRIDGE TO POTTY TRAINING.

The biggest bridge from EC to potty trained is your child learning their own cues rather than you picking up on them. Most parents have the easiest time approaching this as soon as the child has mastered walking. You can still use this book but remember, you've been doing blocks 1 through 4 already. Since self-initiation takes about three to eight weeks from your start date, I'd say that gives you a good gauge of how long it should take to teach that.

I'M A SINGLE PARENT AND YOUR BOOK SEEMS TO ADDRESS TWO-PARENT HOUSEHOLDS. HOW IS THIS PROCESS DIFFERENT FOR SINGLE PARENTS?

You'll probably need to take some time off work, especially if you have no help. Please bear in mind that I am and always have been a single mom. It's more about getting the time to do it than anything different about how you approach it.

I PLANNED MY START DATE FOR A MONTH AWAY WHEN I HAVE SOME TIME OFF, BUT NOW MY CHILD IS ASKING TO USE THE POTTY AND SEEMS TO BE DOING IT THEMSELVES.

This is tricky because even rock stars are going to need help. I'd stay afloat as best you can, helping them when they need or want to go and then just kind of ignoring potty training until you have that time off.

MY CHILD IS NOT ASKING TO GO. IT'S ALL ON ME AND PROMPTING.

Much of this answer depends on how long you've been potty training. I often get asked this on day 4. Remember that self-initiation comes three to eight weeks after starting. Episode 7 of the *Oh Crap! Potty Training* podcast addresses this fully.

MY CHILD DRIBBLES ALL DAY LONG. THEY ARE NOT FULL ACCIDENTS. HOW CAN I STOP HIM FROM DRIBBLING?

Dribbles are totally normal and very common. It's important to remember how much control your child is showing with dribbles. They are starting to pee and stopping themselves to get to the potty. *That's great!* Dribbles usually indicate that your child is waiting to see how long he can hold it, an important part of the process. The dribbles will stop. Meanwhile, you can buy old-school training pants that have a triple layer of thickness in the crotch but are underwear. You also want to highlight the good while addressing the bad: "Oops. I'm so glad most of your pee was in the potty. A little is in your pants. Next time, run to the potty when you have the feeling to pee." Do not make a big deal about dribbles and do not call them accidents.

I'M TOO NERVOUS TO TRY NIGHT TRAINING RIGHT AWAY, BUT I'M THINKING ABOUT DOING NAP TRAINING. CAN YOU TELL ME HOW TO NAP TRAIN?

I know that night training can look terrifying at first, and I commend your knowing that you are not ready to jump in. I have many podcasts about night training. However, it is not possible to "nap train." There is nothing we can do to assist the child. (With night training, you will assist by waking them at least once.) We can't wake a napping child. The best thing to do is limit fluids with the upside-down pyramid of fluids: have them pee right before nap and see if they stay dry. If they do stay dry for a few days in a row, I would ditch the nap diaper. But other than that, there isn't any way to solely train for naps.

WHAT DO YOU RECOMMEND FOR POTTYING GEAR?

I recommend the Björn potty chair for its simplicity and low-to-the-ground squat factor. Regardless of what brand you go with, look for one that doesn't have a back. Kids may need to wiggle their bodies around quite a bit at first. I highly discourage the potty chairs with a ton of bells and whistles. This isn't a toy; it's a toilet. A sturdy stool or, better yet, a squat stool like the Squatty Potty will help encourage independent toilet use. Of note, I don't recommend the child version of the Squatty Potty; I've heard from many clients that it's flimsy. I do recommend a travel potty. It's not totally necessary though; many parents just put the regular little potty in the car. Any sort of piddle pads for beds. Brolly sheets come highly mom recommended for waterproof sheets. I recommend a foldable toilet insert (seat reducer) for both at home and travel. There are tons of variations on all these products. A quick Google search will help you determine the best products for your needs. I always recommend plain and functional to help normalize the whole process. Oh! And two-piece pajamas. Also: check out episode 52 of the *Oh Crap! Potty Training* podcast.

OUR HOUSE SETUP IS REALLY POOR, AND THE BATHROOM IS FAR AWAY. WHAT CAN I DO?

Make sure you have plenty of little potty chairs set out. I can't change the layout of your house, so you might be more dependent on the small potties for a while.

CHAPTER 18

The Casual Plan

Over the years, I've had to develop a more casual plan for some clients. Many people experience huge struggles and feel like a slower approach might be better. Some kids seem to really need to come to this milestone more slowly. While I want to honor this, I have to also be clear that I do not think this is the best way to potty train. A big problem is that most kids learn best in an immersion experience, with lots of repetition and consistency. Another problem with casual potty training is that it can extend the process by a long time, sometimes even years. When I hear about a child who has been in potty training for a year plus, I'm like, *What??* Diapers are convenient, and it's really easy to say you're being casual when it's actually for your convenience and ease, which isn't fair to the child. This can send a mixed message that we use the toilet only sometimes, which can hamper the whole process. It's also really easy to just sort of forget about potty training altogether.

The idea with the casual plan is to take potty training MUCH more slowly yet still attend to it in a concerted way. You just want to have markers to keep moving the process forward so you don't let it sort of fade away into the background of life.

This plan doesn't have to look exactly like I've set out here, but it offers a sample time line.

The potty goes in the bathroom and can stay there. This minimizes the chances that it becomes something other than a mini-toilet.

You should work in weeks, so none of the changes are drastic and there's time for the child to acclimate. We are going to set up "try" times. These should be bare-bummed, without a diaper. Your child may pop up. They may not sit. In the first few weeks, they are not expected to pee. I repeat, do not have the expectation that the child will pee in the potty in the first few weeks. We are acclimating the child to regular pee times and the transition to the process of potty training

The Time Line

WEEK 1

Find a very easy try-time. You're setting up one try-time this week, and it's a common one: before bath, while the child is naked and the water is running. Note that this is contingent on the child bathing every day or nearly every day. Here's what you'd say for this try-time: *Okay, I'm peeing in the potty. Okay, your turn to sit and try. Okay, let's wash hands.* Or, *okay, let's get in the bath.*

Another possible easy try-time is at the first diaper change in the morning. Get the child up, take off the diaper, and walk them into the bathroom with you. You sit on the toilet to pee, then say the try-time language to them: *Okay, I'm peeing in the potty. Okay, your turn. Okay, let's wash hands. Okay, let's get dressed.*

WEEK 2

Find a second easy try-time. This week you're doing two try-times every day. Use whichever you didn't use in week 1. Add in before bath, even if bathing isn't daily. A great week 2 try-time is as the child is getting ready for bed. Again, they go to the bathroom with you and sit. Or it could be the morning one when the child is getting dressed for the day.

It is okay if at this point the child is still popping up and down and not really producing or not even sitting. Many kids do nothing for a week or two. That's okay. If you engage, you ruin it. You really want to just move on. Say your try-time language and then let them be, no matter what they do. The try-time should literally take two minutes out of your day.

You should be giving this zero energy, zero praise. The whole goal is making this as positively normal as possible. This is something we do, plain and simple.

Here's what you say during the try-time in a low, matter-of-fact speaking voice, with not a question in your voice: *I'm going to pee. You sit and try. Okay. Let's wash hands.* That's it.

If they don't sit. No comment.

If they say no, no comment.

If they ignore you, don't repeat yourself.

If they sit and don't pee, just say, "Okay, let's wash hands."

Don't try to get them to sit longer.

There is no comment or praise because this is just a regular thing.

This is typically hard for parents. You want a more casual approach but you also feel it's your job to push it a bit. We're not doing that. We're moving in a methodical way, week by week.

So in week 2, you're saying the try-time language twice a day, so fourteen times that week, using consistency and repetition, and your child is seeing you not reacting no matter what they do. That helps a lot. If you comment or try to get a catch, that's engaging and works against the magic of the plan. You want to act like you have the expectation they're going to step up, but then don't react if they do nothing. You don't care. You have to not care about the end result.

WEEK 3

Add in yet another easy try-time. Any easy try-time is going to be when the diaper is changed and there's a transition in the day. Waking up in the morning, going down for naps, waking up from naps, going to bed, changing before leaving the house for something. Those easy catch times are going to be great try-times.

WEEK 4

Another try-time. Again! These should be fast and easy, not prolonged, no more than it would take an adult to sit and pee or poop.

By now usually at least one of the try-times will be yielding a pee. It's okay if it's not, just a heads-up that it should. If you're not seeing any pee catches, then I would coast for a little while and hold with the number of try-times you have built in before adding more.

WEEK 5

Keeping all your good try-times that you've set up, your child should be diaperless for a portion of the day. Depending on the schedule, it can be anytime. It's easier if it's in the morning for a couple of hours (because the child is at their best). Whatever time it is, it needs to be consistent.

The vigilance needs to be high, just like block 1 high. You're looking for pee signals. If you don't think they'll sit on the potty willingly, then you've got your cup ready to catch pee. Granted, it's only a couple of hours a day.

WEEK 6

Increase the diaper-free time by an hour or two or whatever you can do.

WEEK 7

Consider removing the diapers. You can coast for a week or more here if you want, but in order to potty train, the diapers have to come off at some point.

This now gets you to block 1. There must be a weekend, preferably three days in a row, where you pull the plug. The whole goal is to keep moving forward, keep nudging the child toward completion, but again, easing the transition.

The time line can be played with. It can be sped up or stretched out for months. You can coast for a time in any of the weeks with the number of try-times. You don't have to add to it every week if you have an end goal of two or three months from now, so you can play around with the time line. But this style of casual potty training doesn't usually result in you NOT having to do block 1. You will still need to have that weekend where you cross that line, so to speak. By that point, the child is already releasing some of their pee in the potty so it's been normalized.

Mark your calendar and keep some rough notes and ideas of where you are. It really should take about two or three months doing it this way.

A Few Final Thoughts

If things start falling apart or it's not going as planned, try to pinpoint what exactly is going on and where it went wrong. Narrow it down. Most parents get overwhelmed and think, *My kid is just not potty training*. That's rarely true. Usually there's some component that is messing everything up. Try to find it.

When I consult with parents, that's exactly what I do. I strip it all down and try to find and focus on the one thing that's the root of the problem.

Break down the bad and break down the *good* too. Bounce between the blocks if you need to. Nothing is written in stone. Play around with backing off and moving back in with prompting. Also, remember that there's no big finish line. This isn't a contest or a measure of your parenting ability.

Be creative and think on your feet. What works today might not tomorrow, so come up with something new. If you arrive at a unique solution that works for you but you've never heard of anyone else doing it, go for it! Every child and every circumstance is different. Go with the flow. A former client, Diane, was having a hard time getting her son Luke to pee in the potty. Luke loved everything about toilet paper. In a moment of insight, when she knew he had to pee, she put a square of toilet paper in the potty. Luke peed in it! *That's* the kind of thing I'm talking about. A lot of parents get nervous and want to do everything by the book, literally. It's okay to use your own creative ideas if they strike. Just about everything is okay if the pee is landing in the potty and you're not doing anything too weird. I'll leave what constitutes "weird" to your own family parameters.

Let it go! I know all this probably seems overwhelming. Don't worry. It's a lot of information that will become second nature in a short amount of time. Give your child the gift of responsibility and back off. There's a fine line between watching your child and hovering; learn the difference.

And there's a dance and a rhythm to potty training just like everything else. *Find your way.* Take what I've said and make it yours and your child's. Many parents panic that first day. It's okay. Keep going. You might feel like a crappy teacher. Keep going. You might feel as if your kid is being utterly ridiculous about this. Keep going. It's just another milestone—just another something you are teaching your child.

A parting thought: while I have given you the curriculum, YOU ARE THE EXPERT ON YOUR CHILD. You hold the magic keys. And I know you can do it. And I know your kid can do it. I have full faith and confidence in you.

Rock on!

Cheat Sheet for Parents

Reminders of the dos and don'ts of each block.

BLOCK 1: PEEING AND POOPING ON THE POTTY WHILE NAKED, EITHER WITH PROMPTING OR WITHOUT

By far the most nerve-racking days are the first few of potty training. Here's a few reminders for those first days:

- Do *not* be attached to how long this block takes. Usually one to three days but not always.
- Look for *progress, not perfection!*
- Do *not* ask if your child has to go, prompt with a statement, a choice, or a challenge:
  - Be watchful without stalking. *Don't overprompt* or hover. This will create pressure on the child and will backfire in resistance.
- Stay off your phone.
- Use easy, natural catch times (upon waking, before and after sitting, eating, car rides, before nap or bedtime).
- *This is just another thing you are teaching your child.* Lead with confidence, silliness, and creativity.
- Do *not* post on social media. It will undermine your confidence.

- Don't be afraid to use the Red Solo Cup trick.
- *Do not expect* self-initiation. If it happens, wonderful ... but it won't be consistent, so it's unreliable.
- All you are doing is bringing your child from I'm Clueless to I Peed to I'm Peeing to I Have to Go Pee. Look for progress along that time line.
- Do not bribe or try to convince your child to use the potty. Blend it in with other tasks: "Let's clean up your blocks and go potty and wash hands and then eat lunch."

BLOCK 2: PEEING AND POOPING ON THE POTTY, WITH CLOTHES ON (COMMANDO), WITH PROMPTING OR WITHOUT

Remember that block 2 is the *crux* of potty training. Most kids do fine naked; it's putting clothes on that changes everything. For some kids, wetting a couple of pairs of pants is perfectly normal before clicking. But don't let this go on for more than a day or two.

- Use elastic-waist pants for greater independence and because they're *faster* to remove.
- It's okay to bounce between blocks 1 and 2 for a day or two. Get a good pee on the potty and then put some pants on for a while.
- If poop is happening in the pants, go back to block 1.
- Dresses, loose pants, loose shorts are all fine.
- It's okay to take off pants when you see your child's signal.
- Even if your child begins to self-initiate, you should still prompt. Consistent self-initiating should *not* be expected.

- If you are being met with resistance, back off. You are most likely hovering or overprompting.
- Use the throw-away prompt; remind your child to remind herself. "Your potty is right over there. Let me know if you need help when you need it."
- Use the phrase "After you go pee, then we can." *Don't let this slip into bribery.* There's a big difference.

BLOCK 3: PEEING AND POOPING ON THE POTTY IN DIFFERENT SITUATIONS, WITH PROMPTING OR WITHOUT

Yay! Block 3 is all about leaving the house!

Public restrooms can be *scary*! Always get a good pee before leaving the house. Make it part of the leaving ritual. In the early days, build in enough time so you have some wiggle room to get that pee before you leave.

- Have Post-its in your purse to cover the automatic flusher.
- Bring the potty chair in the car so your child has the option to use it in the car if she is freaked out by public restrooms.
- Also carry a foldable insert with you in a Ziploc for reducing public toilet seats.
- If your child is freaked out upon entering a public restroom, abandon the mission. Offer the car potty chair. Do not push this. If this continues, consider earmuffs or concert headphones for a while. Public restrooms are live, meaning the sound bounces around, which can hurt little ears.

CHEAT SHEET FOR PARENTS

- Always show your child where the restroom is, in both public places and friends' houses.

- At events like parties, be vigilant. Excitement, sugar, and more fluids than usual mean you need to be on high alert. (But don't be that psycho mom, okay?)

- If your child can hold it till they get home and there are no accidents, that's awesome. Many adults won't pee or poop outside their own homes either.

- Bring a change of clothes. Keep some extras in the car with some baggies. Accidents can happen to anyone.

- Make peeing upon arrival and/or upon leaving part of your routine.

BLOCK 4: PEEING AND POOPING ON THE POTTY WITH UNDERPANTS ON

You are more than welcome to try undies at any point in time. Undies fit snug around the same muscles as diapers and can activate the muscle memory to just pee.

- If the first day of undies brings on a lot of accidents where there were none, it's cool to hold off a bit more.

- Undies are a great natural consequence. If the child wets them, they must go back to commando as a *learning tool*, but this can be motivating to the child, so use it.

- Buy a size up so the undies are not as snug as the diaper was.

- There is nothing wrong with going commando for a

long time. Many adults don't wear undies. If your child does well with commando, that's fine.

- Boxers work really well.

BLOCK 5: CONSISTENT SELF-INITIATION

Self-initiation is by far the biggest expectation people have in potty training. It is normal and right for your child to need you to help them with potty training. Prompting is a small crutch. Do not remove it too soon.

- Reliable self-initiation usually happens somewhere around three weeks from your start date.
- *It can take longer than that.* Do not stress out unless your child still needs you to prompt every time after a year.
- Because your child self-initiates once doesn't mean they always will. Still be aware of your child's signals and don't be afraid to prompt when needed.

BLOCK 6: NIGHT/NAP TRAINING (UNLESS YOU ARE DOING IT ALL TOGETHER, THEN THIS APPLIES FROM THE GET-GO)

Night training is the most unscientific process ever. Remember that you must usually wake your child at least once in the beginning because ten to twelve hours is a long time not to pee.

- Begin the upside-down pyramid of fluids *before* actually

night training. Once fluids are being monitored, your child very well may start staying dry on their own.

- Night training is *possible* in a crib. But easier in a bed.
- *Two*-piece pajamas!!! Sleep sacks will make night peeing very hard.
- When possible, leave the little potty by the child's bed. We want to give the child every opportunity to do this on their own, if they decide to.
- Don't chase time. If you find you are doing everything possible and there's no discernible pattern, it's okay to rediaper at night for a month or two. While some adjusting of wake-ups may be necessary, don't chase time all night. Try to pick up the child's pattern, if possible.
- Night training is *never* behavior. The child is never manipulating you with peeing in the night.

Don't Panic!

There are some situations that go above and beyond your standard potty training. While these aren't common they aren't rare either. These warrant extra help and I just want you to know that I got you! These include prior or current attempts at potty training that led to:

- crazy, full-blown disasters
- poop withholding
- pee withholding
- struggles at day care
- struggles with neurodivergent kiddos
- any complicated medical issues

As I've mentioned throughout, first and foremost I have the *Oh Crap! Potty Training* podcast and tons of YouTube videos. At jamieglowacki.com, under the Get Help tab, I offer several courses and the ability to book a one-on-one consultant with either myself or certified consultants.

When your child is struggling it can be tempting to think they're not ready but this isn't the case. Most of these issues only get worse over time and working through them is the best thing to do.

It can feel really lonely when everyone around you is having success and your child is having a hard time. I just want you to know . . . you're not alone.

Get help, don't panic, and we'll see you on the flip side of these issues.

INDEX